In the Christian tradition, hope is one of the three theological virtues, perched between faith and love. In this meditative study, Jason Duesing takes us to the heart of biblical hope, grounded in the finished work of Christ and based on the unfailing promises of God. A book of encouragement for every believer.

Timothy George, founding dean
Beeson Divinity School of Samford University
general editor, *Reformation Commentary on Scripture*

Jason Duesing is a man of "mere hope," and now, through this fine book, he points us to similar joy and confidence in Christ. The reader will leave this book both encouraged and emboldened. Get two copies, one for yourself and one for someone you want to bless.

Jason K. Allen, president
Midwestern Baptist Theological Seminary
Kansas City, Missouri

In this book, Jason Duesing skillfully combines Scripture and practical wisdom to provide Christ-centered, life-giving, refreshing hope for everyone who feels discouraged about living in today's scoffing, cynical, faithless culture. I am happy to recommend it.

Wayne Grudem, PhD, research professor of Theology and Biblical Studies, Phoenix Seminary

It's a cynic's world these days, and we Christians must fight not to succumb to its joylessness and despair. In *Mere Hope*, Jason Duesing describes so well the weapon we must wield in the fight: the unwavering hope of Jesus' return. This is a sure and steadfast hope, one that solidified in my heart as I read this gem of a book.

Christine Hoover, author of *Searching For Spring: How God Makes All Things Beautiful in Time* and *Messy Beautiful Friendship*

In a day characterized by confusion, callousness, indifference, and ever-increasing cynicism, Jason Duesing has given us a timely, accessible, and joy-enhancing study of the power of Christian hope. Duesing demonstrates once again why he is considered one of the truly bright lights among Baptist thinkers. Providing various perspectives and vantage points to engage this subject, this well-written book reminds us of the importance of the biblical and theological foundations for hopeful living in our day. Written with conviction, clarity, and informed insight, *Mere Hope* offers an encouraging path forward for renewal among Christ-followers as well as an invitation for others to consider afresh the hope-filled gospel message. Highly recommended!

David S. Dockery, president
Trinity International University

Mere Hope is a great manual for how to live out gospel hope in our world of pain and cynicism. Rather than a "just passing through" mentality, Jason Duesing calls on us to live out a durable hope in Jesus. The scope of this small volume is vast and the pace is swift, as he covers suffering, our cultural worldview, and the depth and joy found in the word *propitiation*. All of these are informed by the hope of the Christian. It's a good read and good for your soul.

Kyle Hoover, lead pastor
Charlottesville Community Church

MERE
HOPE

MERE HOPE

Life in an Age of Cynicism

JASON G. DUESING

B&H
PUBLISHING GROUP
NASHVILLE, TENNESSEE

Copyright © 2018 by Jason G. Duesing
All rights reserved
Printed in the United States of America

978-1-4627-8660-2

Published by B&H Publishing Group
Nashville, Tennessee

Dewey Decimal Classification: 234.2
Subject Heading: HOPE \ GOSPEL \ CHRISTIAN LIFE

Cover design by Ligia Teodosiu. Cover
image © vectorstock/Hydognik

All Scripture is taken from the English Standard Version.
ESV® Text Edition: 2016. Copyright © 2001 by Crossway
Bibles, a publishing ministry of Good News Publishers.

1 2 3 4 5 6 7 • 22 21 20 19 18

To Kalee

Contents

Foreword

by Russell Moore

"I think something is going wrong with the world, and I don't know what it is." I said that sentence to my wife, absentmindedly, as we watched yet another bizarre development happening. I don't remember if it was one more unprecedentedly ridiculous political moment or yet another church scandal. They all tend to blur together after a while. But with my attention distracted, those were the words that emerged from my mind. Sometimes those moments can tell one what one really thinks, more than premeditated words on a page. My wife responded, "Seriously? Of course something is going wrong with the world. That's what you've been teaching and preaching and writing for the past twenty-five or so years." She was right. In the whirl of bad news, I had momentarily forgotten what I'd learned from Genesis and Jesus.

My problem wasn't just one of temporary theological inconsistency. Left to itself, my mentality would have had deep implications for my soul. Unrealistic expectations of this present age lead to a loss of hope, and a loss of hope leads to despair, and despair leads to an "If you can't beat them, join them" conformity to the pattern of the world. That's why this book is so important for all of us right now. Jason Duesing, as a historian and as an experienced Christian leader, is no Bambi-eyed innocent in the face of evil and suffering. His call to hope is not cheap. Instead, this book teaches us to do exactly what the apostle Paul called us to do: to groan deeply at the wreckage of the Fall around us and, at the same time, to look in wonder toward the weight of glory that awaits the new creation to come (Rom. 8:18–39).

Maybe you are reading this now as you live through a time of intense suffering, external or internal. Maybe you are reading this as you seek to shoulder the burden of someone you love who is. Maybe suffering is waiting for you right around the bend of your story, in ways you can't imagine now. The temptation for you, and for me, is to grow cold and cynical, to numb ourselves to pain and, at the same time, to numb ourselves to hope and joy and even love. The songwriter Rich Mullins recognized this tendency when he sang, "The Jordan is waiting for me to cross through; My heart is aging, I can tell." There are many of us with aging hearts, even sometimes in those of you who are still very young.

This book will not take you long to read. Read it slowly. Ask the Spirit as you do to show you things that can help you to remember the hope within you, or to bear witness to that hope with others. You may well find that the conversation Jason Duesing carries on with you in these pages might just be what you need to look soberly on the horror around, and within us. This book might just help you to grieve, but not as those who have no hope (1 Thess. 4:13). And, in so doing, this book just might help you, and me, to embed the gospel in our minds so firmly that we might just hear ourselves saying the words, "I think something is about to go very right for the world, and I know who he is."

Chapter One

Mere Hope Lives

Hope does not put us to shame.

—Romans 5:5

An Emblem of Hope

At the end of the first century, Clement of Rome invoked a curious symbol when describing the resurrection of Jesus Christ. Borrowing from ancient legend—though he clearly thought the creature was real—he described the phoenix as "an emblem of our resurrection."[1] Clement was followed by a second-century catalog of creatures, the *Physiologus* (meaning Naturalist) that included biblical references and commentary for each entry. This work articulated more clearly that the phoenix (like Christ) has the self-sacrificial "power to slay himself and come to life again" and resurrects from the dead "on the third day."[2]

These two appropriations of the bird baptized this myth and led other Christians to employ the symbol for education and edification. In the third century, Tertullian referred to the phoenix as an instrument of general revelation God provided as a "complete and unassailable symbol of our hope" in the resurrection.[3] In the fourth century, Cyril of Jerusalem wrote his *Catechetical Lectures* to train new disciples in the Christian faith. In his lecture on the resurrection he, seemingly believing that the creature exists, though "remote and uncommon," mentions the phoenix also as an example in nature for the unbelieving world to have a symbol of Jesus' own resurrection. He states:

> The bird . . . makes itself a coffin of frankincense and myrrh and other spices, and entering into this when its years are fulfilled, it evidently dies and moulders away. Then from the decayed flesh of the dead bird a worm is engendered, and this worm when grown large is transformed into a bird. . . . Afterwards the aforesaid Phoenix, becoming fledged and a full-grown Phoenix, like the former one, soars up into the air such as it had died, shewing forth to men a most evident resurrection of the dead.[4]

Now, lest we get sidetracked by the Christian usage of a fictional creature, it is helpful to remember the limits of knowledge and etymology in these early centuries. As professor Micah Mattix explains, even though many of these early Christians seem to believe the bird is real, "most of them are less interested in animals as animals and more interested in their symbolic significance."[5] By the Middle Ages the regular use of the phoenix as a Christian "resurrection bird" faded, but throughout other forms of literature,[6] the avian myth appears to convey and remind of Christian hope. To name two of the most popular, in C. S. Lewis's *Chronicles of Narnia*, a phoenix resides in a silver apple tree, the fruit which gives life, in the creator Aslan's garden. And, in the twenty-first century, J. K. Rowling's *Harry Potter* employs a phoenix to convey themes of resurrection, hope, self-sacrifice, and healing.

What I love about the image of a phoenix—and I suspect it is what our friends in the early church loved as well—is that just at the darkest moment, when you think this majestic creature has died or given its life for another, it is reborn, returning to life. Just as Jesus said, "I lay down my life that I may take it up again"

(John 10:17). Only through the death of the phoenix do we see an even more glorious life—through its suffering and demise, it finds victory.

Thus, the Christian use of the phoenix serves as a fitting emblem for what I call mere hope. The foundation of our hope rose from the ashes of death; "something greater than the phoenix is here" (see Matt. 12:41). This mere hope is good news, for ours is a cynical age without much hope.

The Christian use of the phoenix serves as a fitting emblem for what I call mere hope.

An Age of Cynicism

When I was young, faced with washing dishes or some other such chore, my siblings and I would wonder when science would catch science fiction and our home would function like *The Jetsons*, where everything was automated awesomeness. In the decades since then, our world does indeed resemble the dreams of yesterday's science fiction, but it has also traveled further into dystopia. As one columnist wrote, "In contrast to science fiction tales set in fantastical futures on distant planets, dystopian novels take the anxieties of people on earth and amplify them."[7] With instant global interconnectedness alerting us to all forms of tragedy and conflict, our society appears to have defaulted either to resigned despair or distracted indifference. When regularly our leaders disappoint us by their actions and their human flaws are flouted and magnified due to our relentless and merciless scrutiny, it's easy to see why many have come to a collective understanding that no one can stand with a message of hope. Once a small genre of fiction literature, dystopian-themed novels, games, and movies seem now to be the predominant world in which entertainment takes place, and increasingly the real world as well. Hope, rather than dystopia, is the fiction of our day. What happened?

In the process of avoiding the anxiety of a Big Brother governmental takeover like in George Orwell's *1984*, society instead followed Neil Postman's prediction that we would amuse ourselves to death. And, with anxiety and amusement gone, only cynicism remains. In 2015, composer Mohammed Fairouz wrote, "The age of anxiety has given way to the age of cynicism. Among my generation, cynicism is no longer a bad word: it's being celebrated, and it is often mistaken for intelligence." The age of cynicism, Fairouz continues, is where "it is better to be wry and distrustful than to be open and trusting."[8]

Luis Navia, in his critical study of classical cynicism, explains that in modern times a cynical person is:

> someone who rejects ethical values and ideals . . . and who reacts skeptically and sarcastically to even the most innocent and

well-intentioned human actions. For such a person, most if not all human activities are suspect and unworthy of trust, since no one, according to the cynic, ever seeks or pursues anything except for the specific yet often secret purpose of benefitting himself. For the cynic, accordingly, hypocrisy and deceitfulness, primitive selfishness and unbounded egotism, and gross materialism and disguised ruthlessness are the hidden characteristics of all human behavior. Hence, the cynic does not believe in ideals or lofty aspirations, which are in his mind only linguistic and behavioral games promoted for the purpose of manipulating and duping people, or ways to hide the enormous state of confusion that permeates the average human consciousness.[9]

In addition to these active characteristics of a cynical age, I think there are passive characteristics as well. As we have seen, active cynicism is essentially a functional, if not actual, atheism, where the ultimate end is despair and hopelessness. Passive cynicism is subtler, but perhaps more common. Passive cynicism is more of an idle indifference to the world and the people in it. Here the focus is more on oneself and the ultimate end is elusive or even ignored, often reflected in the common vernacular of the day, "whatever." The passive cynic is like the infamous literary figure Don Quixote, who is impulsive, acts without thought to consequence, and can spend time and energy fighting imagined enemies or tilting at windmills. The passive cynic is a day-trader only focusing on or reacting to the temporal, the shiny, or the loud. In either case, the notion of biblical hope is scoffed at or ignored.

However, Christians should take heed, for we, as those living in this world, are prone to bend toward it. Often, the pull toward cynicism is easier to follow than the struggle to resist. Sarcasm comes too easy, complaining is default small-talk, and despair can mark us more than joy. We might refer to the "Evangelical Cynic" to describe the active voice and the "Evangelical Stoic" to describe the passive.

How are we, as Christians, to live in such times? This book is my attempt to answer that question. But first I want to assert, right into the jungle of cynicism that so easily entangles, that mere hope lives.

Mere Hope Lives

"Frodo Lives!" While traveling a New York subway or the sidewalks of London in the 1960s, you might have come across this exclamation written in chalk (or something more permanent)—but like most passersby, you would not have known what it meant. Following the publication of J. R. R. Tolkien's

The Lord of the Rings trilogy in the 1950s, a growing number of readers developed an attachment and affinity for the epic fantasy, but the novels had not yet achieved the widespread success they have today.

The initial rise in popularity came only after paperback versions appeared in the mid-1960s where they quickly assumed the status of bestseller. As they appeared during a turbulent era of nuclear threat, war abroad, civil rights conflict at home, and a general devolution of culture and society, many young people flocked to Middle Earth to assuage their perplexities—and there they found hope.[10] The least likely of main characters, Frodo Baggins, is a diminutive hero reared in a countryside of conflict avoidance. Thrust by providence into a journey of world-saving self-sacrifice, Frodo and his companions see evil undone and good triumph. But not without cost. The wear and tear of goblin gnashing and literal wrestling with the depths of depravity take their toll, and the hero is worse for wear. This leads to his merciful departure at the hands of the saintly elves, where he is transported from the Grey Havens to a heaven of sorts. Because Frodo's journey does not end in physical death, like many others in the story, readers conclude their reading with a shared hope that Frodo lives. In the 1960s, the Tolkien enthusiasts adopted this early meme as a slogan to express their hope and joy in a dark time, and the phrase "Frodo Lives!" was born.[11]

My aim in this book is to remind and establish the certainty that hope still lives. For those in darkness, despairing, discouragement, trials, sufferings, injustice, and any other besetting maladies, hope can be found. Joy can be rediscovered. While the Bible discusses hope in a variety of contexts, and Christians use multiple expressions of hope, I am presenting the term "mere hope" as a helpful perspective for life in an age of cynicism. In addition to exploring the roots of mere hope found in the Bible, I will use illustrations of hope from some helpful conversation partners, known as the Inklings. J. R. R. Tolkien, mentioned above, and his colleague, C. S. Lewis, regularly included the idea of hope in their works and those remain helpful for what I aim to accomplish in this book. To start, here is what I mean by mere hope.

Mere

Perhaps the most famous use of this word in the history of Christianity is C. S. Lewis's employment of it in his book *Mere Christianity* (1952). Yet, this was neither the first time Lewis used the term, nor was he the first to use it in reference to Christianity.[12] Lewis admired Richard Baxter's use of "Meer Christian" in 1680 to assert "nothing but simple Christianity" in an age of growing factions.[13] Lewis used it similarly, happy for prospective readers to think, at first, that his book introduced the very basics of the faith, but he actually sought to put forward "central Christianity," or the very core of the faith.[14]

Writing to explain further what Lewis (and Baxter) meant by the term *mere*, Timothy George explains that their use of mere is an ancient use and does not mean "merely" or "barely," but rather "truly" or "really." George calls this a "thicker kind of mere—not mere as minimal but mere as central, essential."[15]

When thinking about the hope that all Christians share in a cynical age, my aim is not to develop a full "theology of hope,"[16] or address every instance or way in which we think of hope.[17] Instead, I wanted to hone in on the core of Christian hope, the essential facets that help believers live and endure. Hence, like Baxter and Lewis, and in the tradition and approach that Lewis started, I find the thicker kind of *mere* a helpful word for this project.

Hope

The idea of hope is described 146 times in the Old Testament and 108 times in the New Testament.[18] As such, we could fill an entire book this size with definitions and explanations. For the purpose of establishing here what I mean by "mere hope," I want to provide a few definitions that get at the central or essential biblical understanding of hope.

In the most common sense, biblical hope is "a patient, disciplined, confident waiting for and expectation of the Lord as our Savior."[19] J. I. Packer sees the Bible as, "from Genesis to Revelation a book of hope." Here is what he says:

> The first recorded divine promise, that the woman's seed would crush the serpent's head, was a word of hope in the Garden of Eden (Gen. 3:15), and the last recorded

> promise of Jesus, "I am coming soon" (Rev. 22:20), was a word of hope for churches facing persecution. Hebrews 11:1 defines faith in terms of hope ("Now faith is being sure of what we hope for"). Hope, the guaranteed expectation enabling believers to look forward with joy, is in truth one of the great themes of Christianity and one of the supreme gifts of God.[20]

Finally, Lee Strobel describes hope as "the inextinguishable flicker God ignites in our souls to keep us believing in the prevailing power of his light even when we are surrounded by utter darkness."[21]

Mere Hope

The idea of mere hope does not intend to convey every aspect of the biblical doctrine of hope, nor can it. Rather, mere hope conveys the core perspective of hope that all Christians share.

Jesus instructs in Matthew 6:22 that "The eye is the lamp of the body. So, if your eye is healthy, your whole body will be full of light." In other words, it matters where you look and what you see. In this book, I discuss mere hope from the perspective of four directions to look. If where we set our eyes affects our bodies and hearts, I propose that a healthy way to live in an age of cynicism is regularly to look at hope. First, we should "look down" at the foundation of our hope, the good news of the gospel. This is our gospel hope. Second, we should "look in" and find the fountain of our hope, Jesus Christ, the hope within us. He is our living hope. Third, we should "look out" and see the flourishing of our hope, as the hope of the nations is meant to be shared. This is a global hope.

Mere hope conveys the core perspective of hope that all Christians share.

Finally, we should "look up" and see the focus of our hope, a reminder of what is true. This is our future hope. A final chapter will explore how we can live out mere hope in an age of cynicism.

Pilgrim's Companion

John Bunyan, in his allegory of the Christian life, *Pilgrim's Progress*, introduces a character named Hopeful to aid Christian on his journey "from this world to that which is to come."[22] Hopeful is a fellow pilgrim who joins Christian after his earlier companion, Faithful, was martyred. Bunyan describes him in phoenix-like terms as rising out of Faithful's ashes. Hopeful proves a worthy and helpful companion to Christian. When they were imprisoned together in Doubting Castle by the Giant Despair, it is Hopeful's words that helped calm Christian's mind. Later, as they neared the end of the journey and were faced with crossing a deep river in order to enter the gate to the Celestial City, Christian began to despair, and as they waded in, he began to sink. At that moment, Hopeful provides the encouragement that pulls Christian across the finish line: "Be of good cheer, my brother, I feel the bottom, and it is good."[23]

Christian reader, in a cynical age where despair abounds, there is a mere hope that has found the bottom, and it is good. As you read, be of good cheer, for mere hope lives.

Chapter Two

Look Down

Mere Hope's Foundation

We have this as a sure and steadfast anchor of the soul, a hope that enters into the inner place behind the curtain.

—Hebrews 6:19

A Philology Problem

Philip and Carol Zaleski, in their massive book on the Inklings, *The Fellowship*, give this revealing insight into the mind of J. R. R. Tolkien: "People thought Tolkien was joking when he later said that he wrote *The Lord of the Rings* to bring into being a world that might contain [his] Elvish greeting. . . . The remark is witty—but also deadly serious."[1]

J. R. R. Tolkien loved words. As the Zaleskis explain, the sight and sound of words affected him the way colors and light must affect painters or notes and rhythms affect musicians. More than that, he loved the study of words and delighted in philology or "the zone where history, linguistics, and literature meet."[2] He saw language especially, as both a "fallen human instrument and a precious divine gift."[3] On the one hand human misuse of a common language led to judgment after Babel. On the other hand, God spoke the world into existence with words, sent his Son as the Word, and the Spirit breathed perfectly all the words we have in the Bible as Scripture. Thus, the Christian life is a life clothed and shaped by words, even as some of those words require hard work before revealing their full meaning.

When Tolkien, the artist and composer of words, had achieved the invention of several original languages for his amusement and joy, he found he needed a world to house them. The result? The entirety of the fictional environs we know as Middle Earth and its inhabitants. The world of *The Lord of the Rings*—and all its connected words—found their genesis in their creator's love of words.

When I went to graduate school for theological training for ministry, I had only been a Christian for four years. I knew what it meant to be saved but was still working out all the implications. For example, I had come to learn and love the hymn:

Jesus paid it all,
All to Him I owe;
Sin had left a crimson stain,
He washed it white as snow.

But it was not yet clear to me how exactly Jesus washed me white as snow. I knew that Jesus died for my sins, but I don't think I could have told you what happened when he did or how he did it. That is when I discovered I, too, had a philology problem—a problem with words.

As I often tell students, when I arrived at seminary I was like a crumpled up piece of paper—all I needed to know for life and godliness was there on the page—I just needed some instruction and further discipleship to help iron out my many theological wrinkles. Through a combination of class instruction, mentorship from my pastor, and the discovery of a few important books,[4] I came to study the doctrine of the atonement. As I studied, I discovered that at the core of the atonement is a red-hot blazing Bible word: *propitiation*. I did not know this word, but I came to treasure it. As the *ESV Study Bible* simply and helpfully defines it, propitiation is "a sacrifice that bears God's wrath and turns it to favor."

As I studied, I discovered that while the word *propitiation* is used only four times in the New Testament,[5] its impact is tsunamic—the wave-like implications and effects of this aspect of the doctrine of the atonement reach every corner of the Bible. As J. I. Packer says, "Not only does the truth of propitiation lead us to the heart of the New Testament gospel, it also leads us to a vantage point from which we can see the heart of many other things as well."[6]

From this new vantage point grew further understanding and—don't miss the connection between study and practice—a deeper burden for the lost both at home and throughout the world. For an understanding that, on the cross, Jesus took the wrath of God I deserved (Rom. 5:9) and turned it away from me (Rom. 3:25) so I could have his righteousness (2 Cor. 5:21) led to an understanding that he also has turned it away from every human being on the planet (1 John 2:2), and that righteousness is available for all who repent and believe (Phil. 3:9).

Just as Tolkien built an entire world to house his Elvish greeting, so we could argue that our entire world, and certainly our hope, is built on the depths of the gospel contained in this idea of propitiation. This central message of the gospel serves as the bedrock upon which our hope is built. In our task of building a perspective for life in a cynical age, we do well to look down often to remind ourselves of that on which we stand—and lest we have a philology problem of our own, I want to explore further this precious doctrine at the core of our gospel hope. While we could examine any of the four appearances of this term in the New Testament, I would like to use this chapter to zero in on just one verse, Hebrews 2:17. There we will find that the foundation of our hope is a doctrine to know and a doctrine to share.

A Doctrine to Know

> Therefore he had to be made like his brothers in every respect, so that he might become a merciful and faithful high priest in the service of God, to make propitiation for the sins of the people. (Heb. 2:17)

Great debate remains as to who authored the letter to the Hebrews. However, whether it was Paul, Luke, Apollos, or someone lost to history, what is clear is to whom he was writing and why. Hebrews is addressed to Jewish Christians, probably living in Rome, who were facing persecution. To avoid those trials, many appeared on the verge of returning to Judaism and "drifting away" from "the living God" (2:1; 3:12). The author writes to stop this drifting by exhorting (13:22) them to press on to maturity in Christ. He appeals to them by centering his letter on the word *better*, which he uses twelve times. The author aims to show them that since Christ is better and provides a more sure and lasting hope (6:19; 7:19) than any other set of beliefs or religious system, there is no reason to give up hope, even in the midst of persecution.

As we set our sights on what Hebrews says about the work of Christ in the atonement in order to establish the foundation of our hope, we see that the author of Hebrews excels, under the inspiration of the Holy Spirit, in illuminating the connections between what his Jewish hearers know regarding the role of the High Priest and how Jesus fulfills that role. As the puritan John Owen said, "The Jews knew the great work of the high priest was to make atonement, and the Apostle now instructs them in the substance of what before they had attended to in types and shadows."[7] In Hebrews 2:17 alone we see this substance brightly in three declarations about the life and work of Jesus. In part, the declarations shine brightly because they form a chain that cannot tarnish.

In Tolkien's first volume of *The Lord of the Rings*, the fellowship of hobbits, elves, dwarfs, and men were forced at one point to journey in the dark. Traveling under a mountain, rather than over or around, they entered a series of mines. Once the environs of the dwarves, these mines produced many precious metals, but one of the most precious was mithril. As Tolkien explains, mithril "could be beaten like copper and polished like glass; and the Dwarves could make of it a metal, light and yet harder than tempered steel. Its beauty was like to that of common silver, but the beauty of mithril did not tarnish or grow dim."[8] The foundation of our gospel hope is built with a mithril-like chain of beauty and indestructibility, crafted by God himself for the salvation of humankind. Hebrews 2:17 reveals three links in this chain.

Jesus Was Made like His Brothers—Incarnation

The first part of this verse states that Jesus "had to be" made like you and me. The idea here is that a human had to be involved in the atonement for human sin. William Lane describes this as the "element of moral obligation," for only "by standing with others in human solidarity could the transcendent Son of God be qualified to participate in the life of the people as a merciful and faithful high priest."[9] Certainly God, in his infinite wisdom, could have created a world in which the satisfaction for sin could be achieved by other means, but in this world and under the laws and standards that he set within it, the forgiveness "had to be" achieved this way.

In the eleventh century, a scholar from England named Anselm wrote a book asking and answering our question, *Why God Became Man*. Written in the form of a dialogue with his student, Boso, Anselm shows here why Jesus "had to be" made like us in order for God to provide a way of rescue from his own judgment on sin.

Anselm: *[The atonement by which man is saved] cannot be effected, except the price paid to God for the sin of man be something greater than all the universe besides God.*

Boso: *So it appears.*

Anselm: *Moreover, it is necessary that he who can give God anything of his own which is more valuable than all things in the possession of God, must be greater than all else but God himself.*

Boso: *I cannot deny it.*

Anselm: *Therefore none but God can make this satisfaction.*

Boso: *So it appears.*

Anselm: *But none but a man ought to do this, other wise man does not make the satisfaction.*

Boso: *Nothing seems more just.*

> **Anselm:** *If it be necessary, therefore, as it appears, that the heavenly kingdom be made up of men, and this cannot be effected unless the aforesaid satisfaction be made, which none but God can make and none but man ought to make, it is necessary for the God-man to make it.*[10]

John Owen summarizes it well this way, "If Christ had not been a man, he could not have suffered for men, and if he had not been God, his suffering could not have satisfied infinite justice."[11]

But what does it mean that this God-man was "made like" humankind? Christians have discussed the phrase "made like" since the mysteries of Christ were revealed (Col. 1:26) and throughout the first centuries of early Christianity. These discussions often turned into debates, as a handful of thinkers (and instigators) came with novel ideas and questions that challenged what the church held to be true. These challenges led many to seek to formulate an agreed-upon answer to the question: *How can Jesus be both God and man?* The result was a confessional statement adopted in modern-day Istanbul, called the *Chalcedonian Creed* (AD 451). This wonderful statement says, in part,

> [W]e all with one accord teach men to acknowledge one and the same Son, our Lord Jesus Christ, at once complete in Godhead and complete in manhood, truly God and truly man, consisting also of a reasonable soul and body; of one substance with the Father as regards his Godhead, and at the same time of one substance with us as regards his manhood; like us in all respects, apart from sin; . . . one and the same Christ, Son, Lord, Only-begotten, recognized in two natures, without confusion, without change, without division, without separation.[12]

Those four powerful and clear "without" statements at the end sometimes are translated as four adverbs: *inconfusedly, unchangeably, indivisibly, inseparably.* When read aloud, these statements underscore the indestructible truth of the incarnation of Jesus Christ in such a way that really should be sung. For, in refutation of error and all other hopeless religions of man, Christians declare simply, as George Guthrie says, "Jesus really did become human."[13]

Hebrews 2:17 continues to say that Jesus not only became human, he was "made like his brothers in every respect." As if his clothing himself in humanity was not personal enough (John 1:14), Jesus came to identify with humankind as a brother. Earlier in Hebrews 2:11, the author explains that Jesus, as the sanctifier of all who believe, is not ashamed to call Christians, brothers and sisters. As adopted members of a divine family (Gal. 4:5), Jesus shares not only our humanity, but also considers us kin. New Testament scholar A. T. Robertson said of this incredible identification, "Christ, our Elder Brother, resembles us in reality, as we shall resemble him in the end."[14] And the reformer John Calvin said, "[Jesus] not only put on the real flesh of man, but also all those feelings which belong to man."[15]

The personalization of the incarnation—Jesus is our brother—can, at first, seem hard to understand, as we might feel that we under dignify a holy, powerful God by seeing him as "one of us." But, that is the point and the beauty of Christ's humility and sacrifice. He did not merely take on human flesh as a neutral or perfunctory transaction. He became our brother and wants us to identify with him as such—to look up to him and to follow his example, knowing he has endured and can identify with every trial we will face. This wonderful aspect of the incarnation provides the basis for our having actual fellowship with the God of the universe. He took on flesh and came to us as our brother.

Though sympathetic to our temptations and trials as our brother, and inconfusedly and completely human, Jesus Christ maintained an important and vital distinction: he was without sin (Heb. 4:15). While the testimony of all of Scripture confirms this, in Luke 23, an instance where the account of the trial and execution of Jesus is recorded, there are multiple statements affirming his innocence. If ever there were a place to record an infraction, a slight, an error, the record of the most pivotal trial in history would be the place to record such. Yet, Herod says, "nothing deserving death has been done by him" (Luke 23:15). One of the criminals, hanging next to Jesus on the cross, declared, "this man has done nothing wrong" (Luke 23:41), and, after Jesus died, a centurion, an eyewitness to the death, said "Certainly, this man was innocent!" (Luke 23:47). The man in authority, a fellow convict, and a guard, any of whom could have understandably slandered Jesus, had nothing to say but to declare his innocence.

Why, then, did God become man? We have seen why God had to send Jesus as both God and man, and how Jesus was made like humankind in every respect, calling those who would believe brothers and sisters, all while living a perfect and innocent life. But to what end? Why?

In John 3:16, Jesus says that God loved the world in such a way as to make provision for their sin in the face of judgment. Just prior to this, in John 3:14–15, Jesus alludes to the time Moses was instructed by God to craft a bronze serpent-like staff to hold up at a time when the people were dying due to their sin. All who would look to the staff would live (Num. 21:4–9). In the same way, Jesus said, all who look to him, when he is lifted up, will have eternal life (John 3:15). God's love for the world and desire to provide salvation is why God became man. This foundational doctrine, the source of our gospel hope, has served as a core truth that Christians throughout the centuries have sought to explain and expound. In the fourth century, a remarkable North African theologian named Athanasius wrote a short treatise as an "elementary sketch" of faith in Christ wherein he said, "For we were the purpose of [Jesus Christ's] embodiment, and for our salvation he so loved human beings as to come to be and appear in a human body."[16] Put simply, this first incarnational link of our indestructible mithril-like chain of God's plan for salvation is summarized well as "Christ Jesus came into the world to save sinners" (1 Tim. 1:15).

Jesus Became a High Priest—Mediation

As Hebrews 2:17 occurs near the end of the chapter, the author is, in part, in the process of setting up a transition to discuss the priesthood of Jesus Christ at length in Hebrews 4–10. Thus, he introduces here that Jesus, following his incarnation, became a High Priest, and with that we have the second link in our chain. The idea of Jesus as High Priest is connected to identification with humanity, for as we have seen, he serves as the God-man mediator between God and man. The connection of these two links of our mithril-chain is seen here in the words used as well. The clause "so that" speaks to the purpose of Christ's priesthood; that is, that for Jesus to atone for sin and provide a way for God to show his love for the world, he became a man and he became a High Priest.

Later in Hebrews, the author will explain that a high priest is "appointed to act on behalf of men in relation to God, to offer gifts and sacrifices for sins" (5:1). This mediating role is seen most clearly in the Old Testament on the annual Day of Atonement. On that day, the high priest would enter the holiest part of the tabernacle. This was the only day he could come lest he die. The high priest was a man, just like the people, and had sin that needed atonement as well. He would enter and sprinkle blood from an animal sacrifice as a symbolic offering to make atonement for the sins of God's people (Lev. 16). One man represented the entire nation. One man entered the presence of God with blood from an animal substitute. One man made atonement—but it would last only for a year.

In connection with and in contrast to the high priest of the Old Testament, Hebrews 2:17 describes Jesus as a "merciful and faithful" High Priest. As David Allen notes, the reference to Jesus as faithful likely is an allusion to God's promise to Eli that he would raise up a faithful priest (1 Sam. 2:35) prior to the calling of Samuel.[17] Certainly, Jesus is the ultimate fulfillment of the role of the priesthood in the Bible, but these adjectives also describe the way he continues this service. That he is merciful, we've seen in his sympathy that comes from his willingness to take on human flesh. His mercy is also displayed in his role as ongoing advocate and intercessor to God the Father on our behalf (Rom. 8:34). He does all this priestly ministry "in service of God" (Heb. 2:17), and here, perhaps is where we test the strength of our chain. For as 1 Timothy 2:5 says that "there is one mediator between God and men, the man Christ Jesus," we understand that God's plan of salvation and our path of escape from judgment rests in the work, purity, perfection, and integrity of the Mediator. As George Guthrie explains, "The Son had to become human because high priests are taken from among human beings (see Heb. 5:1), and he had to become a high priest in order to offer the ultimate sacrifice for sins."[18] Therefore, for our mithril-like chain of the beautiful and indestructible links of salvation to function as God intended, it now must twist.

Jesus Made a Sacrifice for Sin—Propitiation

Whereas the Old Testament high priest entered a temporal tent on earth, and had to do so annually, to make symbolic atonement for the people, Jesus Christ entered heaven, once for all, "to put away sin by the sacrifice of himself" (Heb. 9:24–26). The God-man, the Mediator, and now the Substitute—our mithril chain of three links is indestructible only because the One who came and stood between God and humankind also took their place and their punishment. This twisting of the chain, this unexpected turn of events is the phoenix-like core of the foundation of mere hope. To understand this foundation upon which we stand and rest, let's look at the final phrase of Hebrews 2:17, "to make propitiation for the sins of the people."

First, as introduced above, propitiation is "a sacrifice that bears God's wrath and turns it to favor." In the New Testament, propitiation is used always to refer to the work of Christ and carries the sense of God working to satisfy his own demands. Martyn Lloyd-Jones explains further, saying that in any propitiatory event, there are four essential elements:

1. An offence to be taken away,
2. A person offended who needs to be pacified,
3. An offending person; a person guilty of the offence,
4. A sacrifice or some other means of making atonement for the offence.[19]

In other ancient literature, or even in the pagan worship described in the Bible, propitiation conveys the idea that humans, the ones who have offended the gods, must offer some kind of sacrifice to avoid judgment or punishment. Hence, you see all manner of objects sacrificed in the hopes that the gods will send rain or stop a famine.[20] But what is remarkable about gospel propitiation is that God himself, the One offended by sin, provides the means of making atonement by offering himself. Think about that: an all-powerful, all-knowing, all-present God could have created another means of salvation, but he decided to sacrifice himself instead. Meditating on this reminds me of when the apostle Paul prays for the Ephesians, that they would "have strength to comprehend with all the saints what is the breadth and length and height and depth, and to know the love of Christ, which surpasses all knowledge." He then inserts a time of praise to God for his ability to "do far more abundantly than all that we ask or think" (Eph. 3:18–20). How wonderful it is, truly, that God, in his goodness and wisdom, "put away sin by the sacrifice of himself" (Heb. 9:26).

Second, the New Testament helps us to understand that the Old Testament sacrificial system did not actually make atonement. Hebrews 10:4 states that it is "impossible for the blood of bulls and goats to take away sins." Instead, when the Old Testament high priest would symbolically make atonement, he was only delaying the full punishment that would one day be poured out on Christ. When the people of God grew impatient with God and Moses and created their own golden calf to worship (Exod. 32), instead of pouring out his justified wrath, God relents. Romans 3:25 tells us that God, "in his divine forbearance," passed over these sins and others like them to point to the day when he would put forth his Son as a propitiatory sacrifice so that he could both uphold his justice and simultaneously provide justification for the sins of the world (1 John 2:2).

In the twentieth century, but in other times as well, various experts have suggested that the term *propitiation* is too weighty. They prefer to translate the original word as "expiation." The idea here is that clearly humankind has sin that needs forgiveness and removal, but propitiation goes too far in portraying God as angry or wrathful. Expiation, on the other hand, is a cleansing of the guilt and sin, conferring forgiveness, but not an appeasing of God's wrath. The challenge with this way of thinking is twofold.

First, as Lloyd-Jones says, to use expiation is to ignore the specific context of these verses as well as the entirety of biblical teaching.[21] In just once instance, Romans 5:9 says, "Since, therefore, we have now been justified by his blood, much more shall we be saved by him from the wrath of God." The God of the Bible, of both the Old Testament and the New Testament, is a God of wrath and grace—but while we have a clear understanding of what grace is (though one can never think too deeply on this), we are not as clear as to the biblical meaning of wrath. As Leon Morris said, "The wrath of God is often confused with that irrational passion we so frequently find in man and which was commonly ascribed to heathen deities."[22] Rather, biblical wrath is tied directly to God's zeal for what is right and his deep-seated opposition to evil and sin.[23] As God is light, he cannot tolerate the darkness of sin (1 John 1:5), whether intentional or unintentional (Lev. 4:2). The pureness of his character means he can "by no means clear the guilty" (Exod. 34:7). Therefore, since all of humankind has sinned

(Rom. 3:23) and since sin separates us from God (Isa. 59:2), we deserve and should expect to endure God's wrath. Yet, as we have seen, God's loving character, seen in his mercy, is such that he often would withhold his wrath, delaying for a future payment in full at the cross. Psalm 78:38, in one instance of several, reminds that God, "being compassionate, atoned for their iniquity and did not destroy them; he restrained his anger often and did not stir up all his wrath."

Therefore, and second, to pivot to focus solely on the forgiveness of the sinner in expiation neglects the clear Godward focus of the use of propitiation. The late theologian Roger Nicole said the term *propitiation* "indicates beyond question that the atonement is pointed Godward, that its effects are not merely to influence man in his attitude toward God or to transform the basic disposition of his soul . . . but the removal of God's displeasure with the sinner."[24] Thus, rather than dealing with these troubling theological concerns, some English translations of the Bible, in a noble effort to help readers understand difficult concepts, do not translate this word as "propitiation," but rather simply as "atonement" or "atoning sacrifice." While this is less egregious than the use of "expiation," I think it is still unhelpful at best, as it too fails to convey the full weight of the term and its Godward aspect. Merely to use "atonement," in Hebrews 2:17, for one example, fails to convey, as J. I. Packer explains, that "Christ's death has its effect first on God, who was hereby *propitiated* (or, better, who hereby propitiated himself), and only because it had this effect did it become an overthrowing of the powers of darkness and a revealing of God's seeking and saving love."[25]

Finally, a word should be said about the extent of the application of propitiation. While Jesus Christ made propitiation for the sins of the world (1 John 2:2) in a universal sense, this is not universalism—the belief that every human will be saved from judgment. The atonement made possible the forgiveness of sins, but such is not possible without repentance and faith (John 3:16; Rom. 10:9). The transfer of the righteousness of Christ, only comes to those who have "faith in Jesus" (Rom. 3:26).

In examining the very words of Hebrews 2:17, we have seen how God's plan to make provision for the forgiveness of sin, the foundation of our gospel hope, is forged in a precious chain with a twist. While we can and should grow in our knowledge of how Jesus Christ washed us "white as snow," and I hope this chapter has aided in that growth, it was an entirely different experience for Jesus Christ to have lived through it—and we can and should learn about that as well.

Jesus Suffered in Our Place—Substitution

Reviewing briefly the end of Mark's Gospel, we see that Jesus knew he was born to die for others

(Mark 10:45). And, yet, when that time was at hand, the God-man experienced the weight of his death both as God and man. Praying in Gethsemane, Jesus was "sorrowful" (Mark 14:34) and asked God the Father to remove "this cup" from him (Mark 14:36).

What was the cup? Throughout the Bible, "the cup" symbolizes one's God-determined path in life. Psalm 16:5 says, "The Lord is my chosen portion and my cup; you hold my lot." The cup can serve as a picture of salvation (Ps. 116:13) or a reminder of redemption through judgment, as in the Lord's Supper (Matt. 26:27; 1 Cor. 10). However, more commonly, the cup is a symbol purely of suffering and judgment (Ps. 75:8). In several instances in the Old Testament, the cup is referred to as the cup of God's wrath (Isa. 51:17, 22; Jer. 25:15). In the New Testament, the cup foreshadows the specific judgment Jesus will endure (Matt. 20:22; John 18:11), and the final judgment to come (Rev. 14:10; 16:19). Thus, when Jesus asks the

Father to remove the cup, it is not merely a request to avoid physical execution on earth, but rather an understanding that the cup would contain the full wrath God had restrained since the Fall of man. Yet, in submission to the Father, and for his glory, Jesus obeyed and finally preferred God's will and plan, and took the cup.

On the cross, when Jesus cried, "My God, my God, why have you forsaken me?" (Mark 15:34), he is quoting or reciting Psalm 22:1. Wayne Grudem explains, in light of this understanding, that Jesus is not wondering why he is dying, but asking God why he delays in helping him.[26] This is a cry of anguish from the one made "to be sin" for our sake (2 Cor. 5:21). On the cross, Jesus suffered a physical and excruciating execution, but infinitely more severe, he drank the cup of God's wrath and judgment for sin "to the dregs" (Isa. 51:17). In that moment, the perfect and innocent God-man mediated our eternal punishment by taking our place. As John Owen describes, "There was room enough in Christ's breast to receive the points of all the swords that were sharpened by the law against us. And there was strength enough in Christ's shoulders to bear the burden of that curse that was due us."[27] With his last words, "It is finished" (John 19:30), he completed the totality of his propitiation so that there is "now no condemnation for those who are in Christ Jesus" (Rom. 8:1). With his victorious resurrection, Jesus made available his own earned righteousness to all who believe (Phil. 3:9).

With his victorious resurrection, Jesus made available his own earned righteousness to all who believe.

A Doctrine to Share

The solution to our philology problem is found in Christ's death. It's found in the three-link mithril chain of incarnation, mediation, and propitiation. When we understand this, we are able regularly to look down and see, time and time again, the foundation of our hope and the reason for our joy. A marvelous thing happens each time we do, for the core doctrine for *understanding* our gospel hope turns out to be the most important doctrine to fuel an ongoing burden for *sharing* the gospel with others. As John Piper explains:

> No one who enjoys the forgiveness of Jesus can be content to hog it for himself. He is not the propitiation for our sins only. There are other sheep that are scattered throughout the whole world. Their sins, too, are covered. And the last commandment of

> Jesus was, "Go make disciples out of them from every people."[28]

When I come to understand that on the cross Jesus took the wrath of God I deserved (Rom. 5:9) and averted it for me (Rom. 3:25) so I could have his righteousness (2 Cor. 5:21), this unavoidably leads me to an understanding that he also has averted it for every human being on the planet (1 John 2:2), and that righteousness is available for all who repent and believe (Phil. 3:9). In short, the core of our hope is a doctrine to share.

The Foundation of Hope

When I was a young believer in seminary, I knew what it meant to be saved, but was still working out all the implications of my salvation. I had a problem with words—a philology problem. Through my study of the doctrine of propitiation, my young Christian life was transformed as I learned more of the depths and sturdiness of this gospel foundation. Now, almost twenty years later, I return often to this foundation, looking down to remind myself of the hope that resides even in a cynical age.

One other gift I was given in those early years was an entrance into a whole new world of Christian hymns. I didn't grow up regularly attending church, so this was my first chance to learn them. The combination of doctrinal training and learning these songs reinforced my affections for God and his work on our behalf. The hymn that follows is one that I learned in those days, and it fittingly captures the gospel foundation we have explored in this chapter.

"And Can It Be"

And can it be that I should gain
An interest in the Savior's blood?

Died He for me, who caused His pain—
For me, who Him to death pursued?
Amazing love! How can it be,
That Thou, my God, shouldst die for me?

'Tis mystery all: th' Immortal dies:
Who can explore His strange design?
In vain the firstborn seraph tries
To sound the depths of love divine.
'Tis mercy all! Let earth adore,
Let angel minds inquire no more.

He left His Father's throne above
So free, so infinite His grace—
Emptied Himself of all but love,
And bled for Adam's helpless race:
'Tis mercy all, immense and free,
For O my God, it found out me!

Long my imprisoned spirit lay,
Fast bound in sin and nature's night;

LOOK DOWN

Thine eye diffused a quickening ray—
I woke, the dungeon flamed with light;
My chains fell off, my heart was free,
I rose, went forth, and followed Thee.

Still the small inward voice I hear,
That whispers all my sins forgiven;
Still the atoning blood is near,
That quenched the wrath of hostile Heaven.
I feel the life His wounds impart;
I feel the Savior in my heart.

No condemnation now I dread;
Jesus, and all in Him, is mine;
Alive in Him, my living Head,
And clothed in righteousness divine,
Bold I approach th' eternal throne,
And claim the crown, through Christ
my own.

—Charles Wesley (1738)

Chapter Three

Look In

Mere Hope's Fountain

To them God chose to make known . . .
the riches of the glory of this mystery,
which is Christ in you, the hope of glory.
—Colossians 1:27

Till We Have Faces

Just over sixty years ago C. S. Lewis published his last work of fiction—one that he considered "far and away the best that I have written."[1] *Till We Have Faces* is Lewis's retelling of the ancient myth of Cupid and Psyche, though with his own spin. He tells the story from the perspective of Psyche's older sister Orual, who has grown jealous of her sister, as Psyche was taken away by the gods and received blessing and benefit from them. Yet, when Orual attempts to see the gods or the palace where Psyche lives, she can't, and this sets her on a long-term struggle against the gods, and herself.

Lewis uses Orual as a picture of the struggling unbeliever, like a distant relation of Harry Potter's uncle and aunt, Vernon and Petunia Dursley, who cannot, or who refuse to, believe in that which is invisible. Near the end of the story Orual comes to see that she cannot see the gods until she believes. For, as she says, "How can [the gods] meet us face to face till we have faces?" By the end of Lewis's novel, Orual, having wrestled with her struggle of faith in the unseen, comes to a telling conclusion. She says, "I now know, Lord, why you utter no answer. You yourself are the answer."[2]

Belief, trust, and even hope in the unseen dwell at the core of the Christian life, as Hebrews 11:1 reminds us: "Faith is the assurance of things hoped for, the conviction of things not seen." First Corinthians 13:12 adds, "For now we see in a mirror dimly, but then face to face. Now I know in part; then I shall know fully, even as I have been fully known." First John 3:2 says, "Beloved, we are God's children now, and what we will be has not yet appeared; but we know that when he appears we shall be like him, because we shall see him as he is."

C. S. Lewis scholar Louis Markos, commenting on *Till We Have Faces*, adds:

> We are all inbuilt (hard-wired, as it were) with a longing for Goodness, Truth, and Beauty, but we must beware lest we seek them as ends in themselves. . . . When we reject the good, the true, and the beautiful, we grow bent; when we seek them as ends

> in themselves, we stagnate. As long as we remember this, as long as our eyes are drawn heavenward to the One who *is* Goodness, Truth, and Beauty, then shall we all be his bride. Then shall we all be beautiful.[3]

Even though we cannot see God, when we look inward, we can see him, despite ourselves, for he has given us a fountain of living hope through his Word and Spirit. Within us, he is our "hope of glory" (Col. 1:27). Just like Orual, we now see in part; we won't see fully till we have faces.

Therefore, for Christians living in an age of cynicism, it matters greatly where we set our gaze and on what we look to give us proper perspective. We have seen that we are first to look down and remind ourselves regularly of the

It matters greatly where we set our gaze and on what we look to give us proper perspective.

foundation of gospel hope. Likewise, we are to look in and there dwell not on ourselves and our remaining sin, or even things good and true, but on the hope within us, for within resides "Christ Jesus our hope" (1 Tim. 1:1). In a wonderful reflection that helps us understand this personification of hope, Ched Spellman explains:

> Hope in the New Testament is often connected to the resurrection and the life that is found as a result of being "in Christ." . . . Just as Christian hope is only found *in Him*, in a real sense, it ultimately *is Him*. Hope at the most profound level is not an abstract concept but a living person. . . . The highest hope of a believer is Jesus Himself. Thus, holding on to hope involves clinging to the promises and person of Christ.[4]

In days of financial uncertainty, political turmoil, international danger, and the normal challenges of life, clinging to our hope within is the second element of mere hope. We see this clearly in the apostle Peter's explanation of our sustaining living hope in 1 Peter 1:3–9. Peter wrote at the end of his life to "cheer and strengthen" Christians undergoing trials. I hope this journey "looking in" does the same for you.

Hope Within Because He Lives

> Blessed be the God and Father of our Lord Jesus Christ! According to his great mercy, he has caused us to be born again to a living hope through the resurrection of Jesus Christ from the dead, to an inheritance that is imperishable, undefiled, and unfading, kept in heaven for you, who by God's power are being guarded through faith for

> a salvation ready to be revealed in the last time. (1 Pet. 1:3–5)

Have you ever driven by a train and counted each car as you passed? For younger children in our family, that has often been a helpful way to pass the time while on a long road trip—except in West Texas. Out where the deer and the antelope play, one seldom hears any words, nor sees much change in scenery. The endless flatness is only challenged for minimal entertainment value by the longest trains I've ever seen, or attempted to count. When driving alongside these trains, even our most eager counter stopped counting—there were just too many to track or tally.

Like those trains, these verses in 1 Peter represent so much theological and practical truth that we do not have space to tally and examine them all. Yet, for the goal of examining the hope within us, we will stop and open four of them. Peter's train leaves the station by calling the believers he is seeking to encourage to praise God, and all the cars follow in line on the same tracks carrying their theological freight to that end.

Born Again

In the various expressions of contemporary evangelicalism it is often easy to forget that the phrase "born again" is a biblical phrase, and a verb, not an adjective. Peter's use of it here immediately brings to mind the meeting Jesus had with a Pharisee by the cover of night. In John's Gospel, we learn that a ruler of the Jews named Nicodemus came to Jesus to affirm that Jesus knew that he—as a religious leader—understood Jesus was a teacher sent by God. Jesus responded with a statement that only could evoke a question from Nicodemus, rather than more statements. Jesus said, "Truly, truly, I say to you, unless one is born again he cannot see the kingdom of God." Not yet seeing with kingdom eyes, Nicodemus asked two practical and earthly questions about this idea of a second birth: How can a man be born when he is old? Can he enter a second time into his mother's womb and be born? Jesus responded to explain how one can experience birth twice, but that proved enigmatic for the Pharisee, who only could reply, "How can these things be?" (John 3:1–9). Yet, Peter and his readers know the good news that God saves sinners through the life, death, and resurrection of Jesus Christ—and through him we, too, can experience a new birth.[5]

The idea that God has "caused us to be born again" (1 Pet. 1:3) is summarized by the helpful theological term *regeneration*. While most commonly used to refer to the biblical doctrine related to how one is redeemed and given new life, *regeneration* is also a biblical word used in Titus 3:5, "[God] saved us . . . by the washing of regeneration."[6] The confessional statement of my convention of local churches defines regeneration like this:

> Regeneration, or the new birth, is a work of God's grace whereby believers become new

> creatures in Christ Jesus. It is a change of heart wrought by the Holy Spirit through conviction of sin, to which the sinner responds in repentance toward God and faith in the Lord Jesus Christ. Repentance and faith are inseparable experiences of grace.[7]

Two summary statements are in order to allow us to understand and appreciate exactly for what Peter is praising God with this phrase.

First, God is the initiator and author of regeneration. John 1:13 states that children of God "were born, not of blood nor of the will of the flesh nor of the will of man, but of God." Ephesians 2:5 reminds us that we were dead in sin, but God made us alive. Our birth, whether first or second, is not something we can control.

Second, there is mystery in how God regenerates due to our finite and fallen nature. Throughout the Bible and in our own experience we see that people trust Christ for salvation when (1) the gospel is preached, (2) the gospel is heard, and (3) faith is expressed. In several instances, people are commanded to believe: Jesus says, "do this, and you will live" (Luke 10:28), and indicates that "whoever believes" will have eternal life (John 3:16). Paul explains that if you confess with your mouth and believe in your heart, "you will be saved" (Rom. 10:9), and implores men to "be reconciled to God" (2 Cor. 5:20). Finally, Hebrews 7:25 explains that Jesus saves those who "draw near to God through him." At the same time, the Bible conveys that God is at work in all of those instances. We see that God opens hearts (Acts 16:14), uses preaching (1 Pet. 1:12; Rom. 10), and makes one alive (Col. 2:13). In all, therefore, there is great mystery, which is why another one of Jesus' statements to Nicodemus is fitting and helpful. He states that everyone born again by the Spirit is like the wind that "blows where it wishes . . . but you do not know where it comes from or where it goes" (John 3:8). In sum, as we marvel at the goodness of God to "cause us to be born again" (1 Pet. 1:3), it is best to understand regeneration and faith working both simultaneously and instantaneously.

To a Living Hope

The second train car reveals to what we have been born again. Recall that Peter aims to encourage these believers undergoing trials and, thus, as he invites them to bless God with praise, he underscores that they have been given a living hope. Regardless of their present circumstances, these Christians have been regenerated and given a hope that is the very opposite of fear of the future.[8] What does it mean that this hope is alive? Peter adds that the hope comes "through the resurrection" (1 Pet. 1:3), which makes this remarkable series of phrases even more powerful. The hope that is given to believers through regeneration is grounded not merely in a series of propositions about what we can know and read as true—though it is grounded in such. More than merely what we can know, the hope that dwells within us is grounded in the resurrection power of Jesus Christ. As A. T. Robertson shares, "Hope rose up with Christ from the dead."[9] As sure as the grave is empty, our hope is alive—as alive as Jesus.

To an Inheritance

Following this transformative truth, Peter explains that our resurrection-infused hope also gives believers an inheritance. The imagery used here connects to promises in the Old Testament related to a future land for the people of God. Yet, instead of an earthly acreage reclaimed and resettled, the New

As sure as the grave is empty, our hope is alive—as alive as Jesus.

Testament points toward "a better country" that will come in heaven (Heb. 11:16). The promise of a future inheritance kept in heaven "where neither moth nor rust destroys" (Matt. 6:20), would serve to encourage Peter's readers who are exiles and have little hope of returning to their physical home.

To amplify the beauty of their future reward, Peter uses three negative words that help frame the inheritance in terms of what it is not, since what it is defies words.[10] The future reward for believers in heaven is (1) *imperishable.* There is no expiration date and it cannot go unclaimed—it will be waiting for you. (2) The inheritance is *undefiled*, without any blemish, oversight, depletion, or error—it is pristinely preserved for you. (3) What awaits is *unfading.* Whereas the most permanent of memorials or monuments on earth will one day crumble and escape memory, the promises and gifts of God in heaven haven't aged a day (1 Pet. 1:4).

For a Salvation

The final train car reveals that as the future inheritance is secure for exiles born again to a living hope, the exiles themselves are guarded, by God and his power. New Testament scholar Tom Schreiner puts it well, saying that "Peter emphasized in the strongest possible terms the security and certainty of the reward awaiting believers."[11] Further, while we know that God's fortifying his children does not mean exemption from persecution or suffering, what is in view here is the long arc of security the believer has in one day receiving our final, long-awaited inheritance.

In stark and jarring contrast to this heaven-bound freight train of blessing for Christians is the train headed in the opposite direction for those outside of Christ. The Bible makes clear that there are only two types of people in the world, those with this living hope and those without hope and without God (Eph. 2:12). However, as Peter shows, the source of the gifts of faith and hope are God himself—not one's own righteousness or works, for there is no one righteous (Rom. 3:10–11). The good news of the gospel is that while we all were unrighteous in our sin, Christ died for us in order to give us his righteousness (Rom. 5:8). The move from being in a position of judgment under God for your sins to a position of absolution by God because your sins are forgiven through Christ comes only when you have Christ's righteousness (Phil. 3:9). Romans 10:9 says that "if you confess with your mouth that Jesus is Lord and believe in your heart that God raised him from the dead, you will be saved." You will be born again to a living hope.

Hope Within and Suffering

> In this you rejoice, though now for a little while, if necessary, you have been grieved by various trials, so that the tested genuineness

> of your faith—more precious than gold that perishes though it is tested by fire—may be found to result in praise and glory and honor at the revelation of Jesus Christ. Though you have not seen him, you love him. Though you do not now see him, you believe in him and rejoice with joy that is inexpressible and filled with glory, obtaining the outcome of your faith, the salvation of your souls. (1 Pet. 1:6–9)

The year 2016 marked the centennial anniversary of America's National Park Service. In celebration of the anniversary, a particular issue of *National Geographic* contained some amazing photos of several parks—as only *National Geographic* can capture. Now, I pride myself on having a Jed Bartlet-like appreciation for the national parks, so when I looked at these photos, I was captivated. They were unlike anything I had seen. In a single image, you could see both day and night, shadow and light, sun and moon. The photographer, for hours at time, took thousands of pictures, and with the aid of technology, "compressed the best parts into a single photograph." The result is a massive and sweeping image comprised of thousands of smaller photos.[12] Yet, the more I looked, the less certain I was that I liked it. For these photos are attempts at seeing what is not meant to be seen—a full day all at once. The scenery was beautiful, yet odd. It was unnatural. Frankly, it wasn't real.

When we face trials for which we don't know the outcome or don't understand the purpose, and struggle with wanting to know all the answers at once, it is like we are wanting to see a full photo of the end and the beginning, in one frame. But were we to see such, I think we would be disappointed. It likely wouldn't make sense, for it is neither real nor what God intends. God, in his kindness and wisdom and mercy, uses trials and hidden things to draw us closer to himself, and even when we can't understand the outcome or the purpose, joy is revealed in the process.

After Peter reminded his exiled readers that they have a living hope in a God who has saved them and will strengthen and sustain them to the end, he turns to address their trials and suffering.[13]

The End of Suffering

When enduring the onslaughts of a cynical age, we've seen how looking in to find Christ Jesus, our living hope, can not only sustain until the end of time, but also provide strength for the present. Peter rightly acknowledges that this kind of reliance will lead to joy, much like the supportive James 1:2 that instructs believers to "count it all joy" in the face of trials. With the end still in view, Peter also reminds that these trials are only "for a little while" (1 Pet. 1:6). This is not Peter's attempt to minimize them or belittle the pain and challenges they produce, but to offer another bolster of hope that even the longest of trials will, in fact, end. Trials and sufferings are a part of a post-Genesis 3 world. They were not what God intended when he created the world. Whether the result of sin, physical malady, or material loss, trials and sufferings do not escape the believer in Christ (John 16:33) and, indeed, can serve as painful instruments of the evil one.

As we behold and experience the trials that are a shared burden in this world, believers often understandably question why God allows such to happen. Even though God, in his faithfulness and wisdom, may never allow his children to have the full understanding of why he permits suffering, Peter's words here give a great deal of insight and help. Trials, of all kinds, test our faith in crucible-like ways—ways that will show the greatness and goodness of God and result in our greater praise to him. This is, in part, because he endures the trials with us. The living hope we have of Christ himself within us is even better than the appearance of an additional man alongside Daniel's three friends in the fiery furnace (Dan. 3:25). Through Christ, in every trial we have a shield of faith "with which you can extinguish all the flaming darts of the evil one (Eph. 6:16). When we are tempted, God is faithful and "will not let you be tempted beyond your ability, but . . . will also provide the way of escape" (1 Cor. 10:13).

Often the way to rejoicing is the way of weakness through suffering, and a powerful New Testament portrait of this is the life of the apostle Paul revealed in 2 Corinthians. As J. I. Packer explains in is marvelous book *Weakness Is the Way*, the testimony Paul gives shows

> Pain and exhaustion, with ridicule and contempt, all to the nth degree; a tortured state that would drive any ordinary person to long for death, when it would all be over.

> But, says Paul, Christ's messengers are sustained, energized, and empowered, despite these external weakening factors, by a process of daily renewal within.[14]

Paul begins 2 Corinthians declaring that "we felt that we had received the sentence of death. But that was to make us rely not on ourselves but on God who raises the dead" (2 Cor. 1:9). From this reliance comes "good courage" (2 Cor. 5:6) and the ultimate lesson that God's "power is made perfect in weakness" (2 Cor. 12:9).

Packer writes *Weakness Is the Way* from personal experience. He has lived a life of "physical and cognitive weakness" due to a head injury as a child. Yet, Packer's early learning to rely on divine strength has sustained him. Writing in his eighth decade, after recovering from hip replacement surgery, he shares of his growing "acquaintance with Satan's skill in generating gloom and discouragement." Yet, in these years, he reveals, "[m]y appreciation of 2 Corinthians has also grown as I have brooded on the fact that Paul had been there before me. . . . The whole letter is an awesome display of unquenchable love and unconquerable hope."[15] By looking in at Christ Jesus, both Paul and Packer show us the way to the fountain of our hope.

Loving without Seeing

Much like C. S. Lewis's Orual, Peter's readers never saw Jesus in the flesh. Yet, despite their exile, trials, and sufferings, they loved him and believed in him. Peter's commendation of them comes from a man who knew something about faith without seeing. Peter was there when Jesus, in response to Thomas needing to see to believe, said, "Blessed are those who have not seen and yet have believed" (John 20:29). Of course, Peter also knew much about love for Jesus, as part of his early discipleship involved his restoration by Jesus asking him three times about his love (John 21:15–17).

Therefore, when Peter writes of this faith and love resulting in an inexpressible joy (1 Pet. 1:8), he writes of what he knows. When he was with Jesus before the crucifixion, Peter saw him with his eyes, but did not fully love him. Only after the Resurrection, did Peter truly see Jesus with love and joy—and then once Jesus ascended to heaven, Peter continued to love him even without seeing him—to an inexpressible extent.

While the believer's joy may not find adequate words for expression, we can get a glimpse of why by the idea that it is filled with glory. In 2 Corinthians 3, Paul recounts the time Moses came down from the mountain and—his face being filled with glory to such a degree that the Israelites could not look at him—wore a veil (Exod. 34:29–33). Yet Paul says that the Spirit has "even more glory" (v. 8), and believers in Christ are able to "[behold] the glory of the Lord" (v. 18) and will one day see Jesus face to face.

Jesus Christ remained Peter's fountain of hope, even though Jesus was no longer on earth. Thus, Peter relays how much more it is true and possible for other believers to love Jesus without seeing him.

The Fountain of Hope

The personalizing of the exiles' love for Jesus is an important point for establishing the strength that comes when we look in to find our hope. Often, Christians develop their own vocabulary and language for describing how they live the Christian life. Some of this is regional or colloquial, and most of it is helpful in forging an incarnational expression of faith. However, sometimes we fail to talk like the Bible talks regarding our relationship with Jesus Christ. Peter commends his readers' love for Jesus, and I think it's helpful for us simply to express that we love him too. Here is one example of what I mean.

Jared C. Wilson is one of my generation's most gifted writers, and while I enjoy the books that he has written and am always helped by them, it is a short article he wrote that might be my favorite. Sometime in 2013, Jared began a series of tweets that expressed how he felt about his friendship with Jesus, and I suspect that since this is not the typical way we talk, the response was significant. Here are just a few of the statements he wrote:

"Can I Tell You about My Friend Jesus?"

- I love my friend Jesus because he knows everything I've ever thought and still doesn't cross the street to avoid me when he sees me coming.
- I love my friend Jesus because the blood of his sacrifice speaks a better word than the sweat of my effort, and he shouts it triumphantly.

- I love my friend Jesus because he took my death, even though he had plenty of time to think it over and every reason to say no.
- I love my friend Jesus because he never checks his watch while I'm talking to him.
- I love my friend Jesus because he never brings up my old stuff.
- I love my friend Jesus because he keeps the devil on a leash like a dog but will throw him into the lake of fire like he's a cat. #dogperson
- I love my friend Jesus because he doesn't just erase the records against me, he burns the record book and scatters the ashes to nothing.
- I love my friend Jesus because he just straight-up—no hesitations, no qualifications, no ifs, ands, or buts—loves me.
- I love my friend Jesus because while many give me trouble, he gives me rest.

- I love my friend Jesus because he always lives to intercede for me.
- I love my friend Jesus because I can just be myself with him.[16]

In days of financial uncertainty, political turmoil, international danger, or just personal trial, we need this reminder of the relationship we have with Jesus Christ, the fountain of hope living within. As 1 Corinthians 13:12 reminds us: "For now we see in a mirror dimly, but then face to face. Now I know in part; then I shall know fully, even as I have been fully known." Driven by that astounding promise, we persevere through trials that will one day end, knowing that then we will see our friend Jesus face to face. In this we can trust, for hope lives till we have faces.

Chapter Four

Look Out

Mere Hope's Flourishing

"Look, I tell you, lift up your eyes, and see that the fields are white for harvest."

—John 4:35

To Cities of Refuge

A version of the Old Testament Levitical cities of refuge still exist in the world, and people are fleeing to them. They were once set apart for those in need of protection—or at least a fair hearing—so that one may "flee to one of these cities and save his life" (Deut. 4:42). In the twenty-first-century version, many still are coming to save their life, and while there, they are finding life.

Just a few years ago I was walking through the streets of two major global cities, both having been in the news in recent months for acts of terror and political instability. The first in Central Asia was teeming with young professionals and, though centered in a Muslim culture, there were signs that the younger generation in this city were not much different than many in the West in terms of devotion to their historic and national religion. At prescribed times throughout the day, prominent mosques would erupt in amplified calls to prayer. Yet, just as in some of our Western cities where church bells ring out from massive and mostly vacant cathedrals, here the normal course of business is for the people not to pause for genuflection, but to carry on with head bowed toward their smartphone. In the midst of this bustling and burgeoning scene of a transient humanity, there is an underlying great work of God.

In that city, I was visiting a team of college students spending their spring semester serving alongside career missionaries. These students lived and worked every day among local university students, and on the last night I was there, they had an event in the basement of a community center where they regularly invited their new friends to meet and practice their English. In this center, several churches also have their meetings, and it was the event there that night that prompted me to think of the Old Testament cities of refuge. For here beneath this massive city with its clamorous calls to prayer resides a quiet center of refuge—a place where any can come, make friends, improve their English, and hear about the gospel of Christ. Students are coming here, and they are finding life.

The second city I visited is in North Africa. Like the first, this city never sleeps or stops. Indeed, there are few traffic lights; none are needed, for the flow of cars and people lilt like tidal waves at every hour of the day, offering no rest from the tumult. Here another team of college students endured dust, traffic, and the press and noise of the people, as they made a daily trek to their place of service. Taking a combination of metro rail and a mile-and-a-half hike over bridges and under overpasses, along streets without sidewalks, these students were in a daily battle for survival. Yet, they joyfully took on the challenge, for at the end of their trek was another city of refuge. In this metropolis, a displaced people from a neighboring war-torn country has sought a home. At a center for refugees, they daily sought to serve many by lending them aid of all kinds and particularly by teaching them English. After their formal classes, they spent extra time inquiring after their students and gave them lasting words of life. At the time I visited, they had seen two men trust Christ, and students were meeting with them on a regular basis.

Oddly, from these perilous and unstable cities I came home encouraged, for I, too, found refuge. In these cities of great darkness and danger, God is still shining pockets of light and safety for people who have limited or no knowledge of the gospel. For every act of terror in the world today, there are a thousand acts of sacrificial service and gospel proclamation.

For every act of terror in the world today, there are a thousand acts of sacrificial service and gospel proclamation.

God Our Refuge

Often, in our age of cynicism we are much like the psalmist in Psalm 73 who was discouraged and despairing at the seemingly successful state of the wicked around him. So disparaged was the psalmist he almost stumbled in disbelief. The wicked were prospering, living a life of excess and ease. They were like reckless bulldozers steamrolling over their culture—particularly the most vulnerable in that culture—with threats, violence, and bombastic speech. Apparently there was nothing or no one to stop them.

The people of God, on the other hand, were suffering, causing them to falter and to question God's omniscience. How, if God is all-knowing, all-powerful, and good, could such men achieve every end upon which they set their desires? In the midst of these doubts, many of God's people gave in, turning to follow the wicked.

At this point of deep darkness, the burdened psalmist finds new eyes to see. Seeking God, he finds the truth that God still sees and knows. That God will one day act and judge. That in the end, he will set all things right. This knowledge drives the psalmist back to God, where he resolves, "I have made the Lord God my refuge, that I may tell of all your works" (73:28).

Jesus Christ, the True City

In one sense, all of humanity are refugees in search of cities of refuge. All are like sheep gone astray (Isa. 53:6) from our Creator and deserving of judgment. But instead of giving us what we deserved, God judged his Son, so that we would no longer need to flee from him, but could return home to him (Luke 15:20). Jesus Christ is the true City for those "who have fled for refuge" (Heb. 6:18). Thus, the call now is for all to take refuge in God and not fear the temporal evils of man. Whether actual displaced peoples in North Africa or secularized university students in Central Asia, I take courage, for as I saw in the very places that the world would tell us to abandon, people are finding gospel hope. Just as these students left home and studies for the sake of sharing gospel hope, we see another perspective for life in a cynical age. In addition to looking down at our foundation and in at the fountain, we are now to look out and see the flourishing of our hope—for Jesus is the hope of the nations (Rom. 15:12).

As evidenced in the lives of these students, mere hope flourishes when it is employed in the service of others. C. S. Lewis understood this when, in his autobiography, he said, "You cannot hope and also think about hoping at the same moment."[1] What he meant was when our thoughts and affections are truly focused on another, there is no room for self. In *Mere Christianity*, Lewis says something similar of humility. The truly humble man, he says, "will not be thinking about humility: he will not be thinking about himself at all."[2] Looking out to see hope flourish means that, instead of constant introspection, we are seeking to share hope with others.

This is not to say that a perspective of mere hope means we abandon all ambition regarding ourselves. Yes, Romans 12:3 tells not to think too highly of ourselves, but it also says to think of ourselves, and that with "sober judgment." Philippians 2:4 understands that we will, by necessity, look after our own interests, but prioritizes the interests of others. This kind of godly ambition, leveraged for the flourishing of hope, is a powerful thing in an age of cynicism, and the apostle Paul gives a helpful example of it in Romans 15:17–21. Here Paul gives some practical explanations to conclude a letter that really is Paul's systematic theology textbook. After he has explained what the gospel is, Paul says how he intends to come to see these believers in Rome. But he does not plan to stay; rather, he plans to press on and go to Spain. Paul is saying, "I have more work to do. I'm ambitious to do more things." Paul's ambition is not just reserved for Paul; it is an ambition to be shared by all Christians, and it serves as the motivating factor for the flourishing of mere hope.

Ambitious Hope for Those Who Have Heard

> In Christ Jesus, then, I have reason to be proud of my work for God. For I will not venture to speak of anything except what Christ has accomplished through me to bring the Gentiles to obedience—by word and deed, by the power of signs and wonders, by the power of the Spirit of God—so that from Jerusalem and all the way around to Illyricum I have fulfilled the ministry of the gospel of Christ. (Rom. 15:17–19)

First, in Romans 15:17–19 Paul is simply explaining that he has fulfilled the ministry of the gospel where he has most recently served. He begins, however, by doing a unique thing—he boasts. If you know anything about Paul, he has an entire theology about boasting, which is, in short, "don't boast." If Christians are to boast in anything, we are to boast in the Lord (Gal. 6:14). Yet here we find Paul boasting. Why?

He explains through the use of several descriptive phrases that show that his ministry consisted not only in the proclaiming of the Word—although that certainly was the core of what he was doing—but also in showing how he lived his life as he proclaimed the Word. As he references all the supernatural things that God had done to accompany his work and his ministry, Paul is saying that he has every reason to be proud of this work, for God alone has done it.

Of this ministry, Paul concludes with an intriguing statement, saying that now the ministry that he has had over the years has been fulfilled. And just to make clear in what region the ministry is now complete, he gives a geography lesson. He mentions Jerusalem—a city, a town, and a place that hopefully many of us could locate on a map—and then Illyricum—a city, a town, and a place that probably none of us could place on a map. To give some sense of the geographic region he's talking about, imagine taking a map of the Mediterranean Sea and all the countries that surround it and overlaying it on a map of the United States of America. If the location of the city of Atlanta is aligned with the location of Jerusalem, then Illyricum would be the equivalent distance, give or take, of Kansas City, Missouri. Paul is saying the region where his gospel ministry is fulfilled is equivalent to a circle drawn from Atlanta all the way around to Kansas City, as the word he uses for "all the way around" means in a circle. To put it another way, Paul is essentially saying, "The furthest east I have ever been is Jerusalem, and the furthest west I have ever been is Illyricum. All the way around in that circle between these two cities, the ministry has been fulfilled." There he has fully preached the gospel of Christ. How can this be?

The idea here is not that every person in that region, as big as it is, is now a Christian. We know that's not the case. But he is saying that all the people in this region now have access to the gospel. In essence, "I have sown seeds, churches have started, and there now are preachers there who will continue the work; therefore, everyone in this huge region now has access to the gospel of Christ. The gospel has been preached here, the ministry has been fulfilled, and it's now self-sustaining." In our Christian language today we would call this region "reached," and no longer unreached.

Here we see the result of Paul's initial ambition to see gospel hope flourish. As he looked outward considering the interests of those around him, he labored to see the unreached reached with the gospel. This is the same mind-set that now motivates him to move on to those who have not heard.

Ambitious Hope for Those Who Haven't Heard

> Thus I make it my ambition to preach the gospel, not where Christ has already been named, lest I build on someone else's foundation, but as it is written, "Those who have never been told of him will see, and those who have never heard will understand." (Rom. 15:20–21)

Second, in Romans 15:20 we see Paul explain further his desire not to continue to preach where Christ is already named, but to preach where he is not yet known, and here he explains the nature of his ambitious hope. The word *ambition* conveys the idea of "making it his aim." It shows exactly where Paul is focused. The clarifying fact that he is ambitious to "preach the gospel" solidifies the other-centered perspective of his desires. He has personal ambition, to be sure, but at the same time, he is not thinking of himself at all. He knows that the only way people who have not heard the gospel will hear the gospel is if someone goes to tell them (Rom. 10:14–17).

In Romans 15:21, Paul defines his ambition further to show why he is compelled to go to the unreached. He reaches back to the Old Testament to show that it has been God's plan all along to provide the nations with gospel hope. In Isaiah 52–53, the prophet foretells of the suffering servant, the Messiah who will come. Paul is acknowledging that with the coming of Jesus Christ, the day foretold in Isaiah has come and is undergoing fulfillment. Paul explains that those people "who have never been told of" the Messiah will now hear of the Messiah, Jesus Christ.

Under the inspiration of the Holy Spirit, Paul lifts up Isaiah 52:15 and puts it into place in his context, and it drives him to see hope flourish among those who have never heard. This is Paul's ambition.

Given the example and argument of Paul, where does that leave us as we seek to look out to share and see hope flourish? Whereas we have looked down and reminded ourselves of gospel hope, and looked in to see Jesus, to look out means we ask ourselves some questions:

What is your ambition?
Do people have readily available access to the gospel where you live?
Who will go from where you live to reach the people in the world who have never heard the gospel?

To aid us as we think through how our ambition aligns with the ambitious hope of the Bible, here are some contemporary facts.

First, today, the 60 percent of the world that is reached or within reach, houses more than 90 percent of global evangelical missionary efforts.[3] This means that only 10 percent of our missionary force is working among the remaining 40 percent who have never heard the gospel or have little access to the gospel. Further, each year Open Doors International generates their World Watch List to determine the top fifty countries where persecution of Christians for religious reasons is worst. For 2017, the top five countries include: North Korea, Somalia, Afghanistan, Pakistan, and Sudan.[4] When we look at that list in light of where the current evangelical missionary force is deployed, we can draw the following conclusion: in all of those are places where persecution of Christians is the greatest, most people are unreached, and the fewest evangelical missionaries are working. That is an easy-to-see mismatch, and Christians living in reached areas are in the best position to do something about it.[5]

Second, even with advancements in technology and travel, one reason why there still exist many people who have not heard of Jesus Christ is simply because travel to them remains very difficult. However, difficult to reach does not mean unreachable, for many of these have been reached with several twenty-first-century advancements, such as Coca-Cola. An early chairman of Coca-Cola set out as his goal to see a bottle of Coke within "an arm's reach of desire" of every person on the globe. This strategy led to the exponential growth of the company throughout the twentieth century and the virtual fulfillment of that dream by the twenty-first century. While traveling a few years ago among the tribal villages in Madagascar on sandy roads navigating quad-four-wheelers, there was little that reminded me of home in the USA. Stick huts, homemade canoes, and ragged clothing met me in every village. Yet along with these scenes came the familiar red signs with white script announcing the availability of Coca-Cola. Local missionaries told us that in many regions where drivable roads stop, porters are hired to carry Coca-Cola to the remotest villages, proving that if one is committed to achieving his mission in this world, few earthly obstacles remain to prevent it.

The father of modern missions, William Carey, writing in his mobilizing manifesto, *An Enquiry into the Obligations of Christians* recognized even in 1792 the often-unparalleled commitment of commercial enterprise to reach the ends of the earth. Carey noted that if "we should have as much love to the souls of our fellow-creatures, and fellow sinners, as they have for the[ir] profits . . . all these difficulties would be easily surmounted."[6] Thus, while difficulties in travel abound, the unreached for Christ are already reached by many for monetary gain, who come just as far at great expense but not with "good news of great joy that will be for all the people" (Luke 2:10).

At the end of C. S. Lewis's *The Voyage of the Dawn Treader*, the Narnian Prince Caspian asks the boy, Edmund, from England, "It must be exciting to live on a thing like a ball. Have you ever been to the parts where people walk about upside-down?"[7] The mystery of unreached peoples across the globe may, to us, appear as the mysteries of those who "walk about upside-down" to Prince Caspian. Yet we are to take the gospel to them, nonetheless. To those who would rightfully remind those zealous for reaching unreached peoples that there are plenty of lost and even unreached peoples at home, I gladly acknowledge that the call to leave all and go is not universal. However, Romans 15 makes clear that a specific calling exists in the New Testament for believers to see that the gospel is taken to all the peoples of the world. While not the specific vocational call for all believers, all are to contribute to the task. Just as Paul left some like Timothy working behind in the reached areas, many should stay behind today. But, just as Paul sought to enlist those believers in Rome and other cities to aid in reaching the unreached, all should support that ultimate task to see the fulfillment of Psalm 67's prayer for God's saving power to be made known among all nations. In short, some Christians should go and all Christians should support the ongoing work of missionaries across the globe, and especially the parts most in need of the gospel—the places so foreign that it seems as if the "people walk about upside-down."[8]

The Flourishing of Hope

At night, I often find myself singing for joy. My daughter, Lindsey Joy, frightened by the dark or a dream, will call out for me, and I will come to her room, and I will sing for her. I will sing for Lindsey

Joy. And there in the darkness, with the singing, comes peace.

These times with my daughter have helped me understand more how what we do among our churches and seminaries in the States can assist and strengthen the pioneering work among the unreached peoples of the world—a partnership that solidified even more for me during a trip I took to China a few years ago.

Psalm 67 asks God for the praise of the nations, for the ends of the earth to come and praise the one true God. I have prayed, "Let the nations be glad and sing for joy" (v. 4), but until that one evening in China, I had never heard that kind of singing.

When a college friend of mine left for China over fifteen years ago, he went to serve among a minority people group who lived in and around a city surrounded by mountains. The gospel had not yet reached this people, in part, because many of them lived in villages not found on any maps and not readily accessible by any mode of transportation other than foot or bicycle. These people dwelt in a land of deep darkness without any gospel light. So, my friend started on his bicycle, slowly, month by month, attempting to seek and find where all these people lived. At one point, after much effort, he felt he had documented all the known villages of this people residing in the valley area in and around this city.

Days later, setting out to ride up and over one range of mountains, he discovered as he crested the ridgeline another valley spread out before him consisting of dozens of villages never before known, never before reached. Such it is with the pioneering work in China. Incalculable strides made one day are dwarfed the next by the overwhelming sense of how much work remains still to be done.

From the mountains and into those valleys of spiritual darkness, my friend would take the good news of the Lord Jesus, what Ephesians 6:15 calls the "gospel of peace" and we have called gospel hope—two sides of the good news coin. As Isaiah 52:7 reminds, "How beautiful upon the mountains are the feet of him who brings good news, who publishes peace." And as Romans 10 explains, God's plan for reaching these people lost in spiritual darkness and unknown to mapmakers is for someone to carry it to them. Into the darkness came peace. And that is what makes what I heard that night during our trip all the more remarkable.

In the ensuing years since he first arrived in China, my friend and his co-laborers would painstakingly document, map, befriend, learn the language, and share the gospel with the people in the undocumented villages. Today there is a handful of churches among the more than 300,000 people. When I was visiting there, I joined some of these believers for their weekly gathering and listened to them pray and hear from God's Word. To see them meet in secret, care for one another, pray for one another, encourage one another, and treasure their time together was immensely encouraging and humbling; I was looking out and seeing the flourishing of hope in a way I had never before seen or heard.

But of all that I witnessed as I gathered with that church, it was the singing that still echoes in my ears. This was not just any singing; this was praise arising from a people previously unreached with the gospel. These were songs of gladness despite real danger and hardship. I had prayed that God would let people groups like this one find the true peace that only the blood of Christ can provide. Many times I had read Psalm 67 and prayed, but that night was the first time I ever heard a recently unreached people singing with such joy.

At the conclusion of the meeting of this house church, one of the members recounted the marvels of how my friend was the first to bring the gospel to their village; yet, she recognized that the work had only just begun. They had one church, yes, but they did not want to stop until every village has a church, until all have heard. Imagine in that place of darkness hundreds of churches joining that one church in singing for joy and heralding the gospel of peace.

By the grace of God working through local churches, nations of people who have never heard are now hearing. Peoples who have never praised are now singing for joy. Much work remains to be done, and now more than ever do Christians with godly, others-centered ambition need to support this task; but we, too, can sing for joy in the night. For in the darkness, peace is coming, and hope is flourishing.

Chapter Five

Look Up

Mere Hope's Focus

In hope [Abraham] believed against hope . . . fully convinced that God was able to do what he had promised.

—Romans 4:18–21

Keep Calm and Carry On?[1]

At the outbreak of World War II with the imminent threat of German attack felt by many Londoners, the British government sought to inspire and instruct their citizens in their plight of endurance. To avoid paralysis of daily activity or mass hysteria caused by an avalanche of anxiety, the leaders propagated a sloganeering campaign. Perhaps the most popular slogan was "Keep Calm and Carry On" as it resonated well with the stiff-upper-lip constitution of many Britons.[2] The idea of self-reinforced statements to bolster courage and focus energy, especially in the face of danger, is noble and proven effective for wartime morale or even sporting arena triumph. However, for the Christian, the temptation to anchor one's daily faith to self-reinforcement tactics can prove dangerous.

Thus, in an age of cynicism, is it time merely to practice our stiff upper lip and "Keep Calm and Carry On"? Should we circle the wagons of paranoia and fear to bolster strength to ride out a dystopian storm while saying nothing?

In his 1947 classic, *The Uneasy Conscience of Modern Fundamentalism*, Carl F. H. Henry called for "contemporary evangelicalism to reawaken to the relevance of its redemptive message to the global predicament." He believed that the truth was stronger than fiction and that evangelicals had a message for the world. He said, "The message for a decadent modern civilization must ring with the present tense. We must confront the world now with an ethics to make it tremble, and with a dynamic to give it hope."[3] Henry would be devastated if he believed, in any sense, that we have lost focus on this kind of hope.

The "uneasy conscience" of which Henry spoke was the tendency of 1940s fundamentalists to grow uneasy with how to interact with a changing culture and retreat instead of engage. The fundamentalists were not uneasy about the truths of the Bible but rather about how to apply them well to the modern situation. I think for the growing evangelical minority today, the same temptation is present and, not knowing how to withstand the cultural pressures, the easiest thing to do appears to be to worry and retreat. But as Henry said, this mentality leaves no voice "speaking today as Paul would, either at the United Nations sessions, or at labor-management disputes, or in strategic university classrooms whether in Japan or Germany or America."[4] So there is a great need today for Christians living in a cynical age to refocus their hope.

Evangelical Stoicism

The idea of hunkering down in the face of shifting morality is something Martyn Lloyd-Jones likened to the Stoicism referenced in Acts 17. Lloyd-Jones explained that in ancient times,

> The Stoic was a serious and thoughtful man, an honest one who believed in facing the facts of life. Having done so he had come to the conclusion that life is a difficult business and a hard task, and that there is only one way of going through with it and that is that you must exercise firm discipline upon

> yourself. Life, said the Stoic, will come and attack you, it will batter and beat you, and the great art of living, he said, is to remain standing on your feet. And the only way to do it is to brace back your shoulders, to set a firm upper lip, to go in for the philosophy of courage, and say, "I am going to be a man!" . . . You just decide that you are not going to give in, you are not going to be defeated; whatever may happen to you, you are still standing, you are going on and you will stick it to the end. The philosophy of grit, the philosophy of courage, the philosophy of the stiff upper lip.[5]

This kind of Stoicism that is high on morality, asceticism, and indifference, plays well in our day of mutual challenges to "just grind it out." In fact, so prevalent is this mentality even among Christians that there is a version of it we might call Evangelical

Stoicism. Here, we self-philosophize when we counsel to "Remind yourself at all times what you can control and what you can't." Evangelical Stoicism is a philosophy of coping that says, "We cannot control the weather or the economy, but we can control our thoughts and actions." From dieting, to keeping up with technology, to pursuing academic studies, to dealing with trials, to enduring family gatherings or tensions, we easily drift into Stoicism whether we know it or not.

We are quick to medicate, avoid conflict, exaggerate, deflect, blame, and hide. We minimize public embarrassment, overcompensate for errors, redouble our efforts, and study how better to manage our public profile. We are experts at "toughing it out." We read leadership and self-help books about how to succeed, how to press farther. We have gotten very good at being proficient, and we know how to get by.

In the face of the decline of cultural morality we hunker down and huddle up. Yet, simple joy, faith, hope, and thankfulness are conspicuously absent as we "Keep Calm and Carry On."

As we saw in our discussion on trials in the Christian life, this is not to say there isn't any value in perseverance or endurance. Of course, Christ calls us to persevere, to remain steadfast. But often we live as if we are to do much on our own strength, apart from the Spirit. To put it in the terms of what we've examined, when we practice this kind of Stoicism, we are engaging in passive cynicism. Instead of looking down, in, out, or up, we are looking around, failing to rely on mere hope at all.

Simple joy, faith, hope, and thankfulness are conspicuously absent as we "Keep Calm and Carry On."

This is not what Christ meant for us when he said his burden was light (Matt. 11:29–30).

This Evangelical Stoicism on which we often stand just will not do. It is not consistent with gospel hope. As Lloyd-Jones said of Stoicism, "It may be very noble, I will grant you that, but it is noble paganism."[6] In short, "Keep Calm and Carry On" is not a perspective of mere hope. The better way is rooted in focusing our eyes upward on something better than what is found in our shallow pockets of grit and determination. Like C. S. Lewis's famous analogy, we need to cease playing in the mud when a holiday at the sea awaits.[7] To aid us in exploring the focus of mere hope, the apostle Paul shows us how to look up to this future hope in what he recorded in his second letter to his disciple, Timothy.

A Letter from Prison

> Therefore do not be ashamed of the testimony about our Lord, nor of me his prisoner, but share in suffering for the gospel by the power of God, who saved us and called us to a holy calling, not because of our works but because of his own purpose and grace, which he gave us in Christ Jesus before the ages began, and which now has been manifested through the appearing of our Savior Christ Jesus, who abolished death and brought life and immortality to light through the gospel, for which I was appointed a preacher and apostle and teacher, which is why I suffer as I do. (2 Tim. 1:8–12)

Paul's second letter to Timothy in the Bible is believed to be his last. While personalized to Timothy and his work in Ephesus, clearly the teaching of the letter was intended for more readers. At the time of his writing, Paul was in prison likely facing execution, and because of this, as Calvin notes, "all that we read here . . . ought to be viewed by us as written not with ink but with Paul's own blood" for what he was suffering and sacrificing.[8]

Timothy was losing heart, undergoing difficulty, troubled at Paul's arrest, and in need of encouragement. The temptation toward enduring by Stoic hand-wringing must have been strong. Paul, however, was not losing any hope at all, for Paul was no Stoic or Cynic. If you were in prison and facing death, what would your final written letter contain?

In the spring of 1963, Dr. Martin Luther King Jr., president of the Southern Christian Leadership Conference and civil rights leader, was arrested in Birmingham, Alabama. From his jail cell, he wrote a letter especially to his fellow clergymen who preferred he not attempt to advance civil rights as fast as he was. Their passive indifference, their Stoicism (and perhaps Cynicism), if you will, challenged Dr. King, but like Paul, he did not lose hope. In his letter he wrote, "I hope the church as a whole will meet the challenge of this decisive hour. But even if the church does not come to the aid of justice, I have no despair about the future. . . . We will reach the goal of freedom in Birmingham and all over the nation, because the goal of America is freedom."[9] Dr. King was focused on a future hope, not mired in the present circumstances. Indeed, just four months later, he was speaking on the steps of the Lincoln Memorial in Washington, DC, proclaiming his dream that, in part, "my four little children will one day live in a nation where they will not be judged by the color of their skin but by the content of their character. . . . This is our hope. This is the faith that I go back to the South with. With this faith we will be able to hew out of the mountain of despair a stone of hope."[10] Dr. King knew the right focus of hope.

As 2 Timothy marks the last words of Paul written from death row, he is using his final letter to strengthen and provide hope for others. Specifically, in the case of Timothy, he is pleading with him.

A Personal Plea

From his reminder in 2 Timothy 1:7 that God did not give Timothy a "spirit of fear" to the command in 1:8 for Timothy not to be "ashamed of the testimony about our Lord, nor of me his prisoner," we get the picture that Timothy has lost his focus to some degree. Like Peter who, after seeing the wind while walking on the water toward Jesus, began to sink (Matt. 14:30), so Timothy seems to be sinking. When Paul uses the word "ashamed," it could be that he has in mind the words of Jesus in Mark 8:38: "For whoever is ashamed of me and my words in this adulterous and sinful generation, of him will the Son of Man also be ashamed."[11] Therefore, he pleads with Timothy not to be ashamed of two primary things.

Do Not Be Ashamed

First, Timothy should not be ashamed of "the testimony about our Lord" (2 Tim. 1:8). Very simply, Paul is saying, "Timothy, regardless of what comes, whatever happens to me, whatever the authorities do to you or the church, do not be ashamed of the gospel." What a wonderful definition of the gospel is found in this phrase, "the testimony about our Lord."

Second, Timothy should not be ashamed of Paul while he is in prison. But note whose prisoner: Paul states he is the prisoner not of Rome, but of "our Lord." Paul is in prison per the assignment and plans of Christ. Here, Paul is reminding Timothy that no matter what happens in the world, Jesus Christ is still in control of all things and is holding all things together (Col. 1:17). This is no Stoic philosopher or hunkered-down twenty-first-century American evangelical seeking to endure the inevitable; this is a confident, hope-filled Christian, clothed in the armor of God (Eph. 6:10–17).

Share in Suffering

Next, Paul pleads with Timothy to "share in suffering for the gospel" (2 Tim. 2:8). The pioneering New Testament scholar A. T. Robertson believed that Paul coined the Greek word behind this phrase to convey joint suffering for the gospel with both Jesus and Paul. By this Paul reminds Timothy that whatever may come, he is not alone and is not the first to endure the pressures brought by a culture opposed to biblical truth. Further, Paul upholds the legacy of Onesiphorus as an example of this shared suffering. Onesiphorus—perhaps having died in this quest—was not ashamed of Paul or the gospel, and sought to find Paul "earnestly" so he could refresh him in his labors (2 Tim. 1:16–18). This example is in contrast to the two others Paul mentions in 1:15, who were ashamed and who "turned away" from Paul. But the virtue here is not in which individual was stronger or was made of sterner stuff. Paul underscores in 1:8 that suffering done rightly is suffering done "by the power of God." That is, according to the power of God and the strength he provides. This is not suffering by grit. This is not Stoicism. Paul wanted Timothy to share in suffering that was beyond his strength so he could rely on God's power. Timothy was weakening, but God's power "is made perfect in weakness" (2 Cor. 12:9).

How do we share in suffering? Where should the Christian set his focus when faced with opposition to his stand for truth? Practically, the advice of Paul here encourages the Christian to prepare now to suffer, to expect hardship and a culture of opposition to come, so when it arrives you will not be ashamed and not rely on your own Stoic attempts at self-reliance. Further, Paul's admonition encourages the Christian to stand with those who are already suffering.

The core of Paul's plea to Timothy not to be ashamed and to share in suffering is the gospel. In short, Paul is saying to Timothy, "Right living in this world of opposition begins by remembering the gospel." Time spent recollecting the good news is not a vain exercise for the Christian. In fact, it is exactly what the Evangelical Stoic needs. Paul's reminder of the gospel begins, in 2 Timothy 1:9, with the phrase "who saved us and called us to a holy calling." The God who gives power to endure is first the God who saves and calls.

Refocus on the Gospel

Next, Paul states that this salvation from God is "not because of our works but because of his own purpose and grace" (2 Tim. 1:9). The gift of the gospel rests in God's grace so that no one can boast of their own achievement of it (Eph. 2:8–9). This component alone undercuts the idea that we could ever "Keep Calm and Carry On" our way on earth to heaven. Rather, the emphasis of Paul's plea centers on God's gracious purpose in salvation.

God's ways are not ours. He purposes as he pleases, but he is good and so are his purposes. When we talk of God's working in salvation, often great angst ensues. But this need not be the case. We should rather affirm that it is a good thing that God is the author of salvation, for when we pray for God to work in the heart of our neighbor, God can and will. Thus, God's purpose and grace in salvation should be a joyful thing to affirm and even sing. For Timothy, it should have served as a reminder of God's grace to him and also to Paul.

This is not the issuing of the Stoic-prescribed "Think about only what you can control" mantra. Rather, it is, even if we do not understand it, "Remember God is in control!" This is helpfully portrayed in William Cowper's "God Moves in a Mysterious Way."

God moves in a mysterious way
His wonders to perform;
He plants his footsteps in the sea
And rides upon the storm.

Deep in unfathomable mines
Of never-failing skill,
He treasures up his bright designs
And works his sov'reign will.

Ye fearful saints, fresh courage take;
The clouds ye so much dread
Are big with mercy, and shall break
In blessings on your head.

Judge not the Lord by feeble sense,
But trust him for his grace;
Behind a frowning providence
He hides a smiling face.

His purposes will ripen fast,
Unfolding ev'ry hour;
The bud may have a bitter taste,
But sweet will be the flow'r.

Blind unbelief is sure to err
And scan His work in vain;
God is his own interpreter,
And he will make it plain.[12]

Grace was given "before the ages began" (2 Tim. 1:9) and thus is not a new idea or a Plan B recovery. Salvation has been in God's mind since before time and was brought about on his timetable. Because of this we can have confidence that he will bring it to completion on his timetable as well (Phil. 1:6).

Thus, in 2 Timothy 1:10, Paul continues to explain that God's gift of grace "now has been manifested" in the present and here we see, again, that salvation is both beyond time and in time. It is both timeless and timely. Like the conclusion of a long novel, in Colossians 1:26, Paul refers to this work of God as a mystery now revealed. The revelation of salvation came through "our Savior Christ Jesus" (2 Tim. 1:10). His appearing as the incarnated God-man truly is the epicenter of all of history. The Old Testament faithful looked forward to that day and were saved by grace through their faith. All who came and come after look back to that day and are also saved by grace. Looking up at the hope of salvation refocuses the believer on the gospel.

Three Phrases

At this point in his letter, to underscore the importance of his plea for Timothy to remember the gospel,

Paul uses three vital phrases in verse 10 to describe the magnitude of the work of Christ. First, he says Jesus "abolished death." This is the same phrase he uses in 1 Corinthians 15:26, "The last enemy to be destroyed is death," and in Hebrews 2:14–15, when he talks of Jesus destroying "the one who has the power of death." Just as was prophesied in Genesis 3:15, through his death and resurrection, Jesus Christ crushes the serpent, Satan, and brings about the death of death.

Second, Paul states that Jesus "brought life and immortality to light." The idea he conveys here is that of turning on the lights, like in 1 Corinthians 4:5 where light is brought to things "now hidden in darkness," and in Ephesians 1:18 where salvation is described as the enlightenment of the eyes of one's heart. Bringing to light life and immortality is another way of saying unchangeable or immortal life. In contrast to the defeated death of death, Jesus brings the light of immortal life. From God speaking into the darkness in Genesis 1:3 to the Lord God serving as the only light reigning forever in Revelation 22:5, light is used throughout the Bible to show transformed newness.

How these works of eternal weight and infinite size are brought to the likes of Timothy and to us, Paul explains in his third phrase, "through the gospel." Through the gospel, death died and life was illumined. Through the gospel, called, as we saw earlier, the "testimony of the Lord Jesus," man was gloriously reconciled to God. For Timothy, regardless of fears, failures, threats, and pressures, this miraculous good news is worth resting in and singing about. The Stoic and his self-reliance cannot and will not rejoice or focus on this, but the Christian can and should.

Paul's admonition to refocus on the gospel is one that defeats self-reliance, Stoicism, Cynicism, and many other -isms. When we look up at this future hope, we are reminded in the present that we are in need of grace and that we cannot do anything apart from Christ. It should drive us to prayer and daily fellowship with God. It should humble us when in an argument. It should cause us to serve others rather than seek to be served. It should drive us to fight temptation, flee sin, proclaim hope, and seek joy. In short, reminding oneself of the gospel is one of the most practical things one can do.

God Is Able

> But I am not ashamed, for I know whom I have believed, and I am convinced that he is able to guard until that day what has been entrusted to me. (2 Tim. 1:12)

When thinking further about how the Christian should live in our world of rapid social change, we are helped by Paul's second statement of advice to

Timothy. After pleading with him, Paul now shares his conviction that serves as another foundation for his hope regardless of the circumstances. Paul begins verse 12 with a statement referencing back to 1:8 when he essentially says to Timothy, "I told you not to be ashamed of the gospel because I am not ashamed."

Even though he is in prison for his faithfulness to the gospel, he is not ashamed of it. He begins his explanation with the contrasting word, "But," and in just those three letters lies an ocean filled with the fruit of the Spirit. In essence, Paul is saying, "Even though I suffer, even though I am in prison unjustly, even though many have abandoned me, even though this was not my plan . . . *But* I am not ashamed."

In this one word there exists enough joy to fill a jail cell. This one word is broad enough and strong enough on which to build a house of faith and a life of trust. For with this word, Paul is showing how he is, in the words of 1 Peter 4:19, "entrusting his soul to a faithful Creator." No matter what change comes, or what standards of truth fall, Paul is not wringing his hands nor attempting to stir up his own internal strength. For as Paul states, "for I know whom I have believed, and I am convinced" (2 Tim. 1:12).

Paul knows Jesus Christ (Phil. 3:10). He believes in him and trusts him, and this is the model for how the Christian should live. In times of testing and opposition, what you know is important, but even the Evangelical Stoic knows much. More than what is known is *who* is known. Do you know Jesus Christ?

We meet him in his Word and there we are reminded that he is good. He does not lie and he is gracious to his children. In his Word we find truth and strength to resist temptation and fight the evil one. Even when we feel like we are going to break in two, when we come to his Word, we are reminded by him that "a bruised reed he will not break, and a smoldering wick he will not quench" (Matt. 12:20), and that even if you are "so utterly burdened beyond strength [and despair] of life itself . . . that [is] to make [you] rely not on [yourself] but on God who raises the dead" (2 Cor. 1:8–9).

The core of Paul's conviction is that God is able. Here we find this further source of related strength—namely, that God is able. This hope is diametrically opposed to Evangelical Stoicism and the philosophy of "toughing it out." For Paul knows what the Bible affirms over and over again—that we are not able. We are finite creatures, weighed down with the fragilities brought by sin, staring straight into the truth of Jesus' words in John 15:5: "apart from me you can do *nothing*" (emphasis added).

Likewise, the Bible affirms that God is able. For example, when Daniel's three friends refused to worship Nebuchadnezzar's gods and were threatened by him with the furnace of fire, they said, "If this be so, our God whom we serve is able to deliver us from the burning fiery furnace, and he will deliver us out of your hand, O king. But if not, be it known to you, O king, that we will not serve your gods or worship the golden image that you have set up" (Dan. 3:17–18). The God of the Bible is the God who is able "to do far more abundantly than all we ask or think" (Eph. 3:20).

Specifically, Paul is convinced that God is able "to guard until that day what has been entrusted to me" (2 Tim. 1:12). Here he is telling Timothy that the reason he can rejoice and endure is because he knows God is able to protect the most important thing, his future hope in eternal life. When Paul uses the words *guard* and *entrusted*, he conveys the idea of protecting his deposit against robbery. We know from verse 9 that this deposit is namely the gospel of grace given to Paul, that is, his salvation. Paul is certain that God is able to protect his salvation "until that day," the day of Jesus' return. God secured all of this before time began, and thus will guard it until time ends. Thus, all other matters are temporary in comparison.

Paul has seen into the future, and has conviction that is sure. He is convinced God is able. Through the reading of God's Word with the help of the Holy Spirit to look up, we can have the same conviction of hope as Paul. Regardless of the changing moral landscape, the Christian should live with the perspective of rest and contentment in the fact that God is able.

The Focus of Hope

In the last quarter of his life, Carl F. H. Henry observed that, "The evangelical movement looks stronger than in fact it is. . . . But no earthly movement holds the Lion of the Tribe of Judah by the tail. We may need for a season to be encaged in the Lion's den until we recover an apostolic awe of the Risen Christ, the invincible Head of a dependent body sustained by his supernatural power. Apart from life in and by the Spirit we are all pseudo-evangelicals."[13]

Indeed, instead of "The Uneasy Conscience of Modern Fundamentalism" in Henry's day, we wrestle with "The Self-Reliant Conscience of Evangelical Stoicism." Yet, as Paul pleads and reminds, the way to live in a sea of social change is to focus on the hope-filled truth that God is able. As the P. P. Bliss hymn says,

When peace like a river attendeth my way,
When sorrows like sea billows roll,
Whatever my lot, thou has taught me to say,
It is well, it is well, with my soul![14]

For the sporting arena or wartime morale, the Stoicism of "Keep Calm and Carry On" may be a fitting rally cry for victory. But for the advance of the gospel in our hearts, in times of suffering in prison cells around the world, or for just working through how to respond well to changing social standards at home, the "It Is Well, He Is Able" approach might be more revolutionary.

Chapter Six

Living Mere Hope

But this I call to mind,
and therefore I have hope.
—Lamentations 3:21

A Catasterous Disastrophe

"Why shouldn't the bubbles go upward?" Sophie asked.

"I will explain," said the BFG. "But tell me first what name is you calling *your* frobscottle by?"

"One is Coke," Sophie said. "Another is Pepsi. There are lots of them."

"And the bubbles is *all* going up?"

"They all go up," Sophie said.

"Catasterous!" cried the BFG. "Upgoing bubbles is a catasterous disastrophe!"[1]

This exchange from Roald Dahl's children's classic, *The BFG*, brings to light what we often see and feel in our fallen world. Current events, long-standing and systemic sins, and often our own hearts and actions, are frequently wrong-side up and cause more harm than a normal catastrophe. Rather, what we see daily in our age of cynicism is a "catasterous disastrophe"! Dahl's words are clearly made up, but they are close enough to actual words to convey meaning, and they also remind of another word coined by an author.

In 1938, J. R. R. Tolkien published a landmark essay, perhaps his most foundational, "On

Fairy-stories."[2] In it, while seeking to defend the goodness of Happy Endings, he coined the term *eucatastrophe.* A eucatastrophe is built from catastrophe—literally "to turn down"—and the prefix *eu*, meaning "good." Thus, in a story with eucatastrophe, at the point of greatest tragedy, you have the workings also of the greatest good. In a later letter to his son, Tolkien wrote, "I coined the word 'eucatastrophe': the sudden happy turn in a story which pierces you with a joy that brings tears."[3]

What is remarkable about this defining word is that Tolkien meant it, and clearly his works, to "lead us out of literature and into faith."[4] Tolkien said, "In the 'eucatastrophe' we see in a brief vision that the answer may be greater—it may be a far off gleam or echo of *evangelium* in the real world. . . . The Birth of Christ is the eucatastrophe of Man's history. The Resurrection is the eucatastrophe of the Incarnation. This story begins and ends in joy."[5]

To live a life of mere hope is to live knowing that our story ends in joy. To no surprise to you by now, I find Tolkien himself a helpful guide to help us further understanding.

A Eucatastrophe Applied

"I am glad that you are here with me," said Frodo. "Here at the end of all things, Sam."[6] I never expected to get a lesson on living mere hope from the concluding chapters of Tolkien's *The Lord of the Rings*, but I did. The hero and his faithful companion, comprising the remnant of a fellowship that set out on a journey to destroy evil and see the return of their king, lay exhausted and helpless on an erupting mountain of volcanic

> To live a life of mere hope is to live knowing that our story ends in joy.

proportions with no cause for hope of rescue. Yet in that moment they had the peace and security that only victorious soldiers must know when they, though dying, have saved people and nations.

What was their source of hope? Even though the world collapsed around them, they knew that evil was ultimately defeated. Though they expected to die and not find escape, they rested in hope, knowing the truth for which they persevered now reigned. That and remaining fellowship led them to express gladness and joy there "at the end of all things." Of course, as the story goes, the very climax of the eucatastrophe in *The Lord of the Rings* occurs just when it appeared that all hope was lost, as good triumphed in the form of rescuing eagles. The imagery of eagles in Tolkien's work is remarkable for portraying this type of eucatastrophe. In Exodus 19:14, God refers to his deliverance of Israel from Egypt as his bearing them "on eagles' wings." Isaiah 40 speaks of eagles' wings as a source of strength for the weary in a passage that almost depicts Tolkien's scene exactly:

> Even youths shall faint and be weary, and young men shall fall exhausted; but they who wait for the Lord shall renew their strength; they shall mount up with wings like eagles; they shall run and not be weary; they shall walk and not faint. (Isa. 40:30–31)

Of course Frodo and Sam do fall exhausted and are swept up on eagles' wings to safety. When they awake, they find restored fellowship and the return of the king. I never expected to get a lesson on living mere hope from Tolkien's fellowship, but there it was even in *The Lord of the Rings*.

In Tolkien's story, there is great hope and joy for those of us laboring as Christians in an age of cynicism—and thankfully, as we have seen, that is only a reflection of the shining light of truth of these themes found in the Bible. Likewise, in 1 Peter 4:7, the apostle Peter explains that "the end of all things is at hand." By that he means that he and his readers were living in the last days before the return of Jesus. Since that time until our very own, humanity has been living at the verge of the end of the world, but that is not a cause for despair or hand-wringing. Peter's point was focused rather on how one is to live at the end of all things, and he spends the next few verses underscoring this for believers.

Peter explains that while a Christian should have his eyes fixed and his hope set on the soon and certain return of Jesus, he should be using his spiritual gifts, whether serving or speaking, all for the glory of God. What, then, is the source of our hope and on what task are we to have our minds and hearts set? Until the end, whether one eats, drinks, preaches, trains, waters, reaps, types, writes, shares, or disciples, he should be doing these things as the biblically prescribed means for carrying out the Great Commission to the glory of God. Such it is, too, with mere hope. Until Jesus returns, Christians should look down at their foundational gospel hope, look in at their fountain of living hope, look out at the need for a flourishing global hope, and look up and focus on future hope.

Living Mere Hope

As we now bring our journey of examining our mere hope to a close, I conclude with four areas where I think our hope is best expressed. Regularly, we are looking down, in, out, and up as we encounter trials, battle despair, and seek to serve others. As J. I. Packer rightly says, "Hope is a tender plant, easily crushed and extinguished, and every believer must budget for having to battle for it."[7] These four areas are complements to that ongoing part of our Christian life. To put it another way, these are how mere hope is lived.

Remember

In the midst of the destruction of Jerusalem, the author of Lamentations is somehow able to focus on the character and goodness of God. When he does, he has hope (Lam. 3:21). This renewing effect of remembering is something we have been doing throughout this book and it is something regularly practiced throughout the Bible. When Jonah's life was fainting away, he remembered the Lord (Jonah 2:7). On the road to Emmaus, the disciples were helped when they remembered Jesus' words (Luke 24:8). While on earth, Jesus spoke in such a way that his disciples would remember his words when they needed them the most (John 16:4). Whether memorizing Scripture, listening to sermons, or reviewing key Bible passages in times of temptation or need, to live a life of mere hope, the Christian must do the chief work of remembering.

Pray

The author continues in Lamentations 3 to hope in the midst of lament. After remembering, his soul speaks to the Lord, declaring, "great is your faithfulness" and "The LORD is my portion" (Lam. 3:23–24). As Old Testament scholar Heath Thomas says, "The substance of hope in Lamentations is found in the logic of prayer."[8] Even Job, when undergoing his darkest trial and confusion as to the workings of God, indicates that his hope leads to prayer: "Though he slay me, I will hope in him; yet I will argue my ways to his face" (Job 13:15). Mere hope must express itself to God in prayer. The task of remembering to strengthen hope will naturally lead to conversation with God.

Sing

Psalm 149:5 declares, "Let the godly exult in glory; let them sing for joy on their beds." A heart full of joy rooted in mere hope cannot help but express that in praise to God. Singing in bed, or in the privacy of a place or time where no one else knows, hears, or evaluates, is a good indication that mere hope is overflowing. Furthermore, singing or hearing others sing truths about God or praise to God, often has a reorienting effect to "melt the clouds of sin and sadness" and restore joy and hope. Singing to the Lord is a regular command given to God's people throughout the Bible and, when heeded, it serves to ground us in hope, and also stir up hope.

Share

Peter, in his letter to exiles, instructed them to be "prepared to make a defense to anyone who asks you for a reason for the hope that is in you" (1 Pet. 3:15). As we regularly look out toward others in global hope, we will naturally have opportunity to share how God has worked through the gift of mere hope in our lives and in the gospel.

These four areas, while both natural and vital to a healthy Christian life, are deficient if not also practiced corporately with a local church. Mere hope, as the core hope that all believers in Jesus Christ share, is meant to be shared. Not only does this benefit the believer, but it also serves as a biblical vehicle for helping Christians endure the current age of cynicism or whatever might replace it in the years to come.

The Light of Mere Hope and Fellowship in the Darkness

There is a moment in J. R. R. Tolkien's trilogy where his fellowship is faced with the daunting task of traversing the underground mines of Moria. Once a noble and industrious empire of dwarves, Moria now is reduced to something dark and dreadful. Following the leadership of the wizard Gandalf, the company of travelers seek to move quickly and quietly through the darkness—yet without a map. The wisdom of Gandalf manifests itself acutely as he admits that, even though he normally possesses a level of omniscience, he does not know exactly how to proceed. He counsels that before "we make up our minds we ought to look about us."

Not seeing much or many options, the wizard determines that the fellowship should "go towards that light in the north door."[9] The fellowship following the light, however faint, proves essential to their successful navigation, not only through the mines, but also to the achievement of their overarching quest—to see the destruction of evil and the return of their king.

In the real world of the twenty-first century, I liken the Christian's sojourn through our contemporary culture very much to that of the fellowship's journey through the mines. That our culture trends toward that which is dark and dreadful is no surprise or even cause for panic, but knowing how to live as

Christians with a God-given mission in an age of cynicism is often difficult and discouraging.

What is needed are regular sources of light—well-placed windows shining at the right time and to the right degree—that allow those living in the darkness to see, understand, and move more freely in the direction of godliness. Second Peter 1:19 is one of many places in the Bible that reminds that the Word of God itself functions as "a lamp shining in a dark place" for the express purpose of illuminating the Christian traveler's path until "the day dawns and the morning star rises." We have the Bible as a lamp to our feet (Ps. 119:105).

Also, Christians are not meant to traverse this world alone. We are designed to need and require the wisdom that comes from traveling in a fellowship—and the New Testament makes clear that the home base of that fellowship and repository of wisdom is the church (Eph. 3:10). But it is not just a fellowship comprised of brothers and sisters; it is a fellowship joined with the triune God himself (1 John 1:3). God has not left us to plod along alone.

Further, Christians are not merely idle travelers, hunkered down, hoping to reach their destination unscathed and unnoticed. First John 1:7 reminds us that "if we walk in the light, as he is in the light, we have fellowship with one another, and the blood of Jesus his Son cleanses us from all sin." Light gleaned is meant to be light shared (Matt. 5:14–16), and the benefit of grace one receives in salvation is meant to serve as an instrument of transferable good news that calls others met along the journey out from the kingdom of darkness into light (Col. 1:13). We are pilgrim ambassadors of mere hope for Christ.

Tolkien's fellowship, searching for help in a dark corridor, found a faint source of light, and by it, were able to move forward in their quest. As bearers of the light of God's Word, gathered in local church fellowships joined and indwelled by God himself, believers traverse the darkness of an age of cynicism sharing the good news of gospel hope—until evil is destroyed and the King returns. Yes, the greatest eucatastrophe is yet to come, on the wings of a phoenix-like Savior, risen from the dead, and coming soon (Rev. 22:20). Until that day, we live with a mere hope.

Notes

Chapter One

1. *The Ante-Nicene Fathers: Translations of the Writing of the Fathers Down to A.D. 325,* edited by Alexander Roberts and James Donaldson, 1:12

2. "The Phoenix," in *Physiologus* cited in Joseph Nigg, *The Phoenix: An Unnatural Biography of a Mythical Beast* (Chicago, IL: University of Chicago Press, 2016).

3. *The Ante-Nicene Fathers,* 3:554. Tertullian mistakenly translates Psalm 92:12 as "The righteous shall flourish like the phoenix," to support his view of the existence of this bird.

4. *A Selected Library of Nicene and Post-Nicene Fathers of the Christian Church,* edited by Philip Schaff and Henry Wace, 2 7:135–36.

5. Micah Mattix, "Birds of Paradise," in *The Weekly Standard*, March 20, 2017, http://www.weeklystandard.com/birds-of-paradise/article/2007167.

6. See John Milton's *Paradise Lost*, 5:272.

7. Nick Ripatrazone, "The strange hope of dystopian fiction since *The Road*," *The Christian Century*, July 17, 2017, https://www.christiancentury.org/article/strange-hope-dystopian-fiction-road.

8. Mohammed Fairouz, "The Age of Cynicism," *On Being*, July 25, 2015, https://onbeing.org/blog/the-age-of-cynicism/.

9. Luis E. Navia, *Classical Cynicism: A Critical Study* (Westport, CT: Greenwood Press, 1996), 1.

10. Janet Adam Smith, "Does Frodo Live?" in *The New York Review of Books*, 19:10 (December 14, 1972).

11. Humphrey Carpenter, *J. R. R. Tolkien: A Biography* (New York, NY: Houghton Mifflin, 2000), 232–33.

12. Lewis referenced "mere Christianity" in 1942 in his *Screwtape Letters* and his *Preface to Paradise Lost*. In 1944, he mentioned it again in his introduction to a publication of Athanasius's *On the Incarnation*.

13. Richard Baxter, *Church-History of the Government of Bishops and Their Councils* (London, 1680).

14. George Marsden, *C. S. Lewis's Mere Christianity: A Biography* (Princeton: Princeton University Press, 2016), 181–82. It is actually in Lewis's introduction to *On the Incarnation* where he explains that by "mere Christianity" he means "plain, central Christianity."

15. Timothy George, "A Thicker Kind of Mere," in *First Things*, May 18, 2015, https://www.firstthings.com/web-exclusives/2015/05/a-thicker-kind-of-mere.

16. In the 1960s, modern theologian Jürgen Moltmann published *Theology of Hope* (1967). Influenced by philosophers Ernst Bloch and Immanuel Kant (and not as much on biblical revelation), Moltmann started a movement within Lutheranism that emphasized eschatology in an era when such was minimized. Joined by Wolfhart Pannenberg and Carl Braaten, later dubbed

the "Theologians of Hope," their works explored process theology, and attempted to escape theodicy by focusing on what God was doing in the present and not the future. This "theology of hope" was influential for a decade and even inspired the rise of black theology and liberation theology.

17. For helpful and more comprehensive studies on hope, see J. I. Packer and Carolyn Nystrom, *Never Beyond Hope* (Downers Grove, IL: IVP, 2000); Lee Strobel, *The Case for Hope* (Grand Rapids, MI: Zondervan, 2015); Kelly M. Kapic, *Embodied Hope* (Downers Grove, IL: IVP, 2017).

18. "Hope," in *New International Dictionary of New Testament Theology*, 2:238–44.

19. Ibid., 2:243.

20. J. I. Packer and Carolyn Nystrom, *Never Beyond Hope*, 14.

21. Strobel, *The Case for Hope*, 2.

22. John Bunyan, *Pilgrim's Progress* (1678), updated and edited by C. J. Lovik (Wheaton, IL: Crossway, 2009).

23. Ibid.

NOTES

Chapter Two

1. Phillip Zaleski and Carol Zaleski, *The Fellowship: The Literary Lives of the Inklings* (New York, NY: Farrar, Straus and Giroux, 2015), 26.

2. Ibid., 24.

3. Ibid.

4. In particular, J. I. Packer, *Knowing God* (Downers Grove, IL: IVP, 1993) and Leon Morris, *The Apostolic Preaching of the Cross* (Grand Rapids, MI: Eerdmans, 1955).

5. Romans 3:25; Hebrews 2:17; 1 John 2:2; 4:10.

6. J. I. Packer, "The Heart of the Gospel," in Packer and Mark Dever, *In My Place Condemned He Stood* (Wheaton, IL: Crossway, 2008), 42.

7. John Owen, *Epistle to the Hebrews* (Grand Rapids, MI: Kregel, 1990), 37.

8. J. R. R. Tolkein, *The Fellowship of the Rings: Being the First Part of The Lord of the Rings* (Wilmington, MA: Mariner Books, 2005).

9. William L. Lane, *Hebrews 1–8, Word Biblical Commentary*, Vol. 47A (Grand Rapids, MI: Zondervan, 2015), 64.

10. Anselm, *Why God Became Man*, 2:6.

11. John Owen, *Communion with God* (Edinburgh: The Banner of Truth Trust, 1991), 66.

12. "The Chalcedonian Creed," in Justin S. Holcomb, *Know the Creeds and Councils* (Grand Rapids, MI: Zondervan, 2014), 56.

13. George H. Guthrie, *The NIV Application Commentary* (Grand Rapids, MI: Zondervan, 1998), 116.

14. A. T. Robertson, *Word Pictures in the New Testament* (Nashville, TN: Broadman, 1930), 5:350.

15. John Calvin, *Calvin's Commentaries*, Vol. 22 (Grand Rapids, MI: Baker, 1996), 74.

16. Athanasius, *On the Incarnation* (St. Vladimirs Seminary Press, 2012), 4.

17. David Allen, *Hebrews, New American Commentary* (Nashville, TN: B&H Publishing Group, 2010), 223.

18. Guthrie, *The NIV Application Commentary*, 111.

19. Martyn Lloyd-Jones, "Propitiation" in *Romans: Atonement and Justification, An Exposition of Chapters 3.20–4.25* (Banner of Truth, 1970), 70.

20. John Stott, *The Cross of Christ* (Downers Grove, IL: IVP, 2006), 171.

21. Lloyd-Jones, "Propitiation," 73.

22. Morris, *The Apostolic Preaching of the Cross*, 149.

23. Ibid., 209, and Lloyd-Jones, "Propitiation," 75.

24. Roger Nicole, "C. H. Dodd and the Doctrine of Propitiation," *Westminster Theological Journal* 17:2 (May 1955): 117–57.

25. J. I. Packer, "What Did the Cross Achieve? The Logic of Penal Substitution," in Packer and Mark Dever, *In My Place Condemned He Stood*, 72.

26. Wayne Grudem, *Systematic Theology* (Grand Rapids, MI: Zondervan, 1994), 576.

27. Owen, *Communion with God*, 66.

28. John Piper, "Jesus Christ Is an Advocate for Sinners," February 10, 1985 (Minneapolis, MN: Desiring God), http://www.desiringgod.org/messages/jesus-christ-is-an-advocate-for-sinners.

Chapter Three

1. C. S. Lewis to Mrs. Anne Scott, 26 August 1960 in *Letters of C. S. Lewis* (New York, NY: Harcourt Brace, 1966, 1988), 492.

2. C. S. Lewis, *Till We Have Faces: A Myth Retold* (London: Harcourt, 1956), 308.

3. Louis Markos, *Restoring Beauty* (Downers Grove, IL: IVP, 2010), 58.

4. Ched Spellman, "When Hope Screams," in *Southwestern Journal of Theology* 53:2 (Spring 2011): 113–14.

5. Peter uses the phrase "born again" in 1 Peter 1:23 as well. For a wonderful exploration of the gospel along the lines of this definition, see Jared C. Wilson, *Gospel Deeps* (Wheaton, IL: Crossway, 2012), 21 and following.

6. For a helpful introduction, see Matthew Barrett, *What Is Regeneration?* (Phillipsburg, NJ: P&R, 2013).

7. "Article IV. Salvation," *The Baptist Faith & Message, 2000.*

8. Paige Patterson, *The Pilgrim Priesthood* (Eugene, OR: Wipf and Stock, 2004), 31.

9. A. T. Robertson, *Word Pictures in the New Testament* (Nashville, TN: Broadman, 1930), 6:81.

10. Patterson, *The Pilgrim Priesthood.*

11. Tom Schreiner, *1, 2 Peter, Jude, New American Commentary* (Nashville, TN: B&H Publishing Group, 2003), 63.

12. Patricia Edmonds, "Photography That Layers Time," *National Geographic* 229:1 (Jan. 2016): 144.

13. A. T. Robertson, *Word Pictures in the New Testament*, 6:75.

14. J. I. Packer, *Weakness Is the Way* (Wheaton, IL: Crossway, 2013), 99–101.

15. Ibid.

16. Jared C. Wilson, "Can I Tell You about My Friend Jesus?" *The Gospel Coalition*, September 16, 2013, https://blogs.thegospelcoalition.org/gospeldrivenchurch/2013/09/16/can-i-tell-you-about-my-friend-jesus/.

Chapter Four

1. C. S. Lewis, *Surprised by Joy* (Orlando, FL: Harcourt, 1955), 211.

2. C. S. Lewis, *Mere Christianity* (San Francisco, CA: HarperSanFrancisco, 2001), 114.

3. For these facts and further commentary, see Jason G. Duesing, "The Pastor as Missionary," in Jason K. Allen, ed., *Portraits of a Pastor* (Chicago, IL: Moody, 2017), and "Status of World Evangelization 2017," Joshua Project, available from http://joshuaproject.net/assets/media/handouts/status-of-world-evangelization.pdf.

4. "World Watch List," Open Doors International, available from https://www.opendoorsusa.org/christian-persecution/world-watch-list/.

5. In addition to a mismatch of sent personnel, there is also the mismatch of resources. In my own missions-focused denomination, the Southern Baptist Convention, for example, in 2014–2015 the 46,793 churches reported total resources of $11.5 billion. Of that number, a total of $227 million was reported as money designated to fund global missions. While that is an astounding number, and reflective of a heart for the peoples of the world, it remains only 2% of our total resources. Available from http://www.sbcec.org/bor/2016/2016SBCAnnual.pdf.

6. William Carey, *An Enquiry into the Obligations of Christians to Use Means for the Conversion of the Heathens* (1792), 69.

7. C. S. Lewis, *The Voyage of the Dawn Treader* (New York, NY: Harper Collins, 1952; 1998), 225.

8. This paragraph is adapted from Jason G. Duesing, "The Pastor as Missionary," in Jason K. Allen, ed., *Portraits of a Pastor* (Chicago, IL: Moody, 2017).

Chapter Five

1. Portions of this chapter are adapted from Jason G. Duesing, "How Should the Christian Live?" in *Gospel for Life: Same-Sex Marriage,* Russell D. Moore and Andrew T. Walker, eds. (Nashville, TN: B&H Publishing Group, 2016).

2. "So what is this 'Keep Calm and Carry On' thing all about then?" at http://www.keepcalmandcarryon.com/history/.

3. Carl F. H. Henry, *The Uneasy Conscience of Modern Fundamentalism* (Wheaton, IL: Crossway, 1947, 2003), 53–55.

4. Ibid., 25.

5. Martyn Lloyd-Jones, *I Am Not Ashamed: Advice to Timothy* (Grand Rapids, MI: Baker, 1986), 15.

6. Ibid., 33.

7. C. S. Lewis, *The Weight of Glory and Other Addresses* (New York, NY: Harper Collins, 1949, 1976, 1980), 26.

8. John Calvin, *Commentaries on the Epistles to Timothy, Titus, and Philemon* (Grand Rapids, MI: Baker, 2003), 179.

9. Martin Luther King Jr., "Letter from a Birmingham Jail," in Bryan Loritts, ed., *Letters to a Birmingham Jail* (Chicago, IL: Moody, 2014), 36.

10. Martin Luther King, Jr., "I Have a Dream," in James Melvin Washington, ed., *A Testament of Hope* (San Francisco, CA: Harper San Francisco, 1991), 219.

11. Such is the suggestion of A. T. Robertson in his *Word Pictures in the New Testament* (Nashville, TN: Broadman, 1930), 4:612.

12. William Cowper, "God Moves in a Mysterious Way" in John Newton, *Olney Hymns in Three Books* (London, 1824), 199–200.

13. Carl F. H. Henry, *Confessions of a Theologian* (Waco, TX: Word, 1986), 390.

14. P. P. Bliss, "It Is Well with My Soul," in Ira David Sankey and P. P. Bliss, *Gospel Hymns*, No. 2 (Cincinnati, OH: John Church, 1895), 412. See also Lloyd-Jones' use of this in *I Am Not Ashamed*, 20.

Chapter Six

1. Roald Dahl, *The BFG* (New York, NY: Puffin, 1982, 2007), 66.

2. J. R. R. Tolkien, "On Fairy-stories," in C. S. Lewis, ed., *Essays Presented to Charles Williams* (Oxford: OUP, 1947; Grand Rapids, MI: Eerdmans, 1966), 90–105. See also Verlyn Flieger and Douglas A. Anderson, eds., *Tolkien on Fairy-stories* (London: Harper Collins, 2014), 119.

3. J. R. R. Tolkien, *The Letters of J. R. R. Tolkien* (New York, NY: Houghton Mifflin Harcourt, 2000), 100.

4. Phillip Zaleski and Carol Zaleski, *The Fellowship* (New York: NY, Farrar, Straus and Giroux, 2015), 246.

5. Tolkien, "On Fairy-stories," 83.

6. J. R. R. Tolkein, *The Return of the King: Being the Third Part of The Lord of the Rings* (Wilmington, MA: Mariner Books, 2012).

7. J. I. Packer and Carolyn Nystrom, *Never Beyond Hope* (Downers Grove, IL: IVP, 2000), 18.

8. Heath Thomas, "'I Will Hope in Him': Theology and Hope in Lamentations," in Jamie A. Grant, Alison Lo, and Gordon J. Wenham, eds., *A God of Faithfulness* (London: T&T Clark, 2011), 220.

9. J. R. R. Tolkein, *The Fellowship of the Rings: Being the First Part of The Lord of the Rings* (Wilmington, MA: Mariner Books, 2005).